The Isle of Man
by tram, tr… t

T

Edited by: Miles Cowsill

Copyright: Stan Basnett

Photography by: Stan Basnett & Lily Publications.

First published by Leading Edge Press 1990
Second edition published by Leading Edge Press 1992
Third (revised) edition published by Lily Publications Ltd 2006
Forth (revised) edition published by Lily Publications Ltd 2012

Published by Lily Publications Ltd., PO Box 33, Ramsey, Isle of Man, IM99 4LP
Tel: +44 (0)1624 898446, Fax: +44 (0)1624 898449.
www.lilypublications.co.uk EMail: lilypubs@manx.net

ISBN 987-1-907945-13-7

CONTENTS

FOREWORD

The first edition of Tram, Train and Foot was published by Leading Edge Press in 1990, with a second edition following two years later. When Lily Publications approached me with a view to doing a third reprint I soon realised that the Island had changed dramatically in the last decade, indeed so much so that not only was a revision necessary but in some cases a complete re-write of some of the walks would be required.

Together with my wife Carol, we set about walking the paths again to see just how much had changed and both realised how change is a continuous process and living with it we don't appreciate just how much things have altered. The Mannin Infirmary and Ballamona Hospital, formerly the Lunatic Asylum, are no longer there. The Majestic, Douglas Bay and Douglas Head hotels have been demolished and replaced by apartments, as indeed have so many of the former hotels and boarding houses on Douglas Promenade. Summerland has been demolished and the face of Douglas changed forever.

Large new industrial estates have sprung up where there was once a relatively rural walk. Pulrose has changed and the power station with its unusual chimney has altered once again. Mentioning chimneys, there is also the new incinerator with its dramatic chimney. There is the new harbour lifting bridge at Douglas and its associated water retention scheme. A similar retention scheme at Peel has a new bridge linking East Quay to the Castle and so on.

Whilst this has always been the case it is just that the pace of change has increased. The face of many rural areas has similarly been changed. Accordingly the walks as described are a snapshot of the Island as it is now. The original concept of the walks described in the first edition set about looking back at our industrial past and comparing with the present.

This edition continues that theme, concentrating on the Island's industrial past and comparing it with the present. The opportunity has been taken also to revise many of the photographs and expand on this theme which is very much part of our Island heritage.

Port Soderick

Much of the mining and quarrying information is taken from The Geology of the Isle of Man by G W Lamplugh and a survey of remains at Laxey by the Institute of Archaeological Research. Place names are from Place Names of the Isle of Man by J J Kneen. Measurements used in connection with mining and the railways have been retained in imperial measurement as conversion to metric is meaningless in context.

Stan Basnett
April 2012

INTRODUCTION
SETTING THE SCENE

The physical features of the Isle of Man as we see them today were formed at the end of the Ice Age as the ice sheet retreated. The pre-Cambrian rocks were ground to their present smooth rounded profile as the ice slowly melted. The glens of the Island were gouged out by the meltwater as it rushed to the sea. The flatter alluvial plains of the north and south were formed as the detritus from the ice was deposited.

The first inhabitants of the Island were Bronze Age people who have left their mark. Standing stones and flint remains tell us that people from the Mesolithic age were present on what was later to become Mann. They were followed by Neolithic Man and Neolithic monuments, stone circles and long barrows can be seen at the Meayll or Mull Hill *(meaning bare or bald hill)* at Cregneash, Cashtal yn Ard *(castle of the height)* in Maughold, several sites in Lonan and at other locations in the Island where modern names such as the Giant's Grave have hidden their true origins. To find out more you should visit the Manx National Museum in Douglas where there are a number of presentations which will without doubt satisfy the more curious.

They were followed by Celts who had migrated into Europe from about the 6th

Port Soderick

century BC from S W Germany, bringing with them a culture still to be traced in the Scottish Hebrides and Highlands, the Isle of Man, Wales, Cornwall and Brittany. They eventually reached Mann and they too have left their mark still to be seen to the present day. The earthwork remains of their great roundhouses at Ballanorris, *(Norris's homestead)* the Braaid *(a gorge)* and Ballakeighan *(Mac Akoen's farm)* bear silent witness to their one - time presence, as do their many promontory forts often built on areas of previous occupation. They also endowed the Island with traditions and folklore which are still remembered to the present day by many Manx folk, perhaps the most famous being the legend of Mannin McLir the Celtic Sea God who lived on the Island and who held the magic property of being able to shield his Island home in mist to protect it from invasion by other deities.

The Celts were farmers and tribal by nature and established a form of land tenure, much of which has survived to the present day with the use of treens and quarterlands as divisions of land. There are places in the Island now where quarterland boundaries can still be seen marked by large white stones, the significance of which is gradually being lost. Their period of occupation was one of prosperity and peace. A visit to the House of Manannan at Peel is a must to discover more about this period of history.

Then came the Vikings but the Manx were not inclined to give in easily to their several attempts at occupying the Island and it was only after several bloody battles that the Vikings could lay claim to Mann. In 1079 Godred Crovan made a landfall at Ramsey in the north of the Island and attacked the Manx, defeating them in a bloody battle at the end of which the Manx suffering many casualties surrendered and begged for mercy. The battle took place on the slopes of Scacafell or Sky Hill *(its Norse name was Skogarfjall meaning wooded hill)* not far from the ancient landing place at the mouth of the Sulby River.

The Vikings were to have a profound effect on the Island, so much of which has survived to the present day. They introduced a form of Government, the origins of which

IMR No.4 Loch emerging from Crogga Glen with a southbound train

The Great Laxey Mine Railway

can be traced to the date when they fought and conquered the Manx. The Vikings had come by way of the western isles of Scotland. These islands were divided into the northern group - the Nordreys - and the southern group - the Sudreys. The kingdom of Mann and the Isles included the Sudreys or more correctly the Sudr-evjar. The Vikings also had a presence in York and in Dublin and at one time ruled the Island from there. It is only here and in Iceland that their spirit is perpetuated in common everyday forms of Government and place names outside of their native country.

Their practice was to assemble their freemen at a meeting field within their area once a year at midsummer and proclaim the law (the so-called breast law) one to another. Such courts were known in Norse as the thing. They survive in Mann as Tynwald *(Thingvollr the Parliament field)* and in Iceland as the Althing *(Althing the Parliament field)*. The Icelandic Parliament dates from 930 AD, making it the oldest Parliament in the world. The Manx Parliament dates from 1079 AD and still to this day follows the principles laid down by the Viking settlers.

Our independence from the rest of the British Isles remains to this day and gives the Island the ability to control its own economy. The Island was used during the eighteenth and nineteenth centuries as a back door entry to Britain for brandy and other goods from the continent that carried heavy tax duties. Smuggling, or the 'trade' as it was known, was a lucrative business for everyone from the individual boatman to the wealthy merchant but the Island eventually came under the control of the Crown. A visit to Castle Rushen and the National Museum in Douglas will elaborate on this early history for those who are interested and the story is worth exploring.

Then came the industrial revolution and the Island had its own fair share of entrepreneurs who saw opportunities, not all of which were successful, followed by the boom in holiday traffic, particularly from the North of England. Even as late as the 1950s the Tourist Board used the slogan 'Come abroad to the Isle of Man'. The advent of cheap flights to sunnier places put an end to all of that. Our walks will touch on most of these aspects as we explore the Island.

The Victorians described the Isle of Man as 'the gem of the Irish Sea' and so it was, for it was they who developed it as a popular watering place. It became the playground of the North West of England, served by a comprehensive network of sea routes by which thousands of people travelled to the Island for their summer holidays. If Blackpool was the 'Costa del Sol' then the Isle of Man was the 'Majorca' of the period.

Many of the rail and tram relics which can be seen on the Island owe their existence to this holiday trade and will form the basic framework of our walks around the Isle of Man.

It is quite difficult to believe now but travelling between the various towns and villages of the Island was extremely arduous in the middle of the nineteenth century. Castletown was the capital of the Island at that time and Douglas was expanding rapidly as a centre of culture and trade attracting merchants and gentry. It became the centre for smuggling, particularly tobacco, brandy and rum due to advantageous rates of taxes payable to the Lord of Mann, as opposed to England - but that is another story.

To illustrate the difficulties, there is documented evidence of a fire which occurred at King William's College in 1844 to which a battalion of men were sent from the Castle in Castletown. The fire was intense and a messenger was sent on horseback to Douglas to summon the help of the Sun fire engine. The engine was immediately despatched to Castletown, taking almost six hours to get there due to the condition of the roads, which were muddy and deeply rutted.

More roads were laid out by the Disafforesting Commissioners in 1860 and

Ramsey bound train at Gob y Deigan in 1965

many of these form the basis of the present network of roads in the Island. It was not until 1923 that any significant improvement in the running surfaces of the rural roads was made. This was considerably later than the rest of the British Isles, with perhaps the exception of Ireland and the remoter parts of Scotland.

RAILWAY MANIA

It is not surprising, therefore, that when the railway mania hit Britain there was considerable interest in the promotion of a number of railways in the Isle of Man at the same time. A number of these early schemes came to nothing, but in 1870 the Isle of Man Railway Company was formed. The Company promoted the building of lines to connect Douglas to Castletown, Peel and Ramsey.

With a registered capital of £200,000, and only £30,000 subscribed by 1872, the promoters faced real problems. The Ramsey line was dropped from the scheme and Sir John Pender and the Duke of Sutherland, who became Chairman in 1872, joined the directors. Under their guidance and influence the Company gained strength and stature. Work was commenced on the line from Douglas to Peel and the first train ran on 1st May 1873, pulled by a 2-4-0 tank engine which had been named SUTHERLAND and was built that year by Beyer Peacock & Company of Manchester. It was the forerunner of a successful class of engine which has provided faithful service to the present day. This locomotive has been restored to service and can occasionally be seen in action in the summer months.

The official opening ceremony took place on 1st July 1873 with full ceremonial. While the Peel line flourished, work continued on construction of the line to serve the south of the Island. This line was completed the following year and opened to traffic on 2nd August 1874 from Douglas to Port Erin. The Company by this time operated five locomotives and fifty coaches and wagons.

By 1870 the Island had entered a period of rapid expansion and most of the hotels that form the façade of Douglas Promenade were built between this date and 1900 to cater for

No.1 Sutherland photographed at Quarterbridge during 1873

the rapid rise in holiday traffic, which by 1890 had reached 275,500.

Ramsey felt badly done to having been left out of the Isle of Man Railway Company plans. Not surprisingly, a group of distinguished gentlemen with interests in Ramsey and the north of the Island promoted the Manx Northern Railway Company Ltd. registered in 1877 with a capital of £90,000. This too proved to be a difficult sum to raise in such a small Island.

However, raise it they did and on 23rd September 1879 the first train entered service with little or no celebration. The line had been built between Ramsey and St. Johns, where a terminus was built adjoining the Isle of Man Railway Company halt with a physical connection to the Peel to Douglas line, but without running rights. By 1880 the Manx Northern extended a line from their station at Ramsey as a tramway serving the quay at Ramsey harbour; the Company at this time operating three locomotives: The first two were built by Sharp Stewart and Company Limited and the third by Beyer Peacock to exactly the same design as the IMR engines; all were 2-4-0 tank engines. At this time only the latter carried the name THORNHILL. The two earlier engines were later named RAMSEY and NORTHERN in 1893.

The Foxdale mines, which were amongst the most productive of any in the British Isles, were attractive to both the IMR and the MNR for the haulage of ore and the Manx Northern had an advantage with their quayside tramway. But the ore had to be moved by horse-drawn cart to St. Johns for onward shipment and competition was fierce. Both companies had a desire to build a connection in the form of a branch line to connect Foxdale to their own line.

In the end, a separate company, the Foxdale Railway Company, was formed to build the two and a half mile branch line to connect Foxdale to St. Johns and the MNR line. Funding was achieved with considerable difficulty and an agreement was entered into whereby the MNR undertook to operate the service. This arrangement would eventually lead to the downfall of the Manx Northern, but not before the Island saw the arrival of the largest locomotive ever to operate on the Island's railways.

It was a six coupled locomotive built by Dubs and Company of Glasgow and it was needed to handle the heavy freight traffic on the predominantly 1:50 gradient of the Foxdale line. It became MNR No.4 and carried the name CALEDONIA. All of this activity made St. Johns the Crewe junction of the Isle of Man but apart from the former Manx Northern station building, which remains as a private house, little now remains to give a clue to the activity of the place in its heyday. In 1903 the whole of the steam railway network was taken over by the Isle of Man Railway Company on the authority of the Insular Government.

One other branch line remained to be built. During the 1914-18 war, an internment camp was built on farmland at Knockaloe in Patrick, near Peel, to house some 20,000 persons. A branch line to serve this camp was built from a junction near Glenfaba Mill for approximately one mile to Knockaloe Camp. There was an associated siding on Peel Quay. The whole branch was built for the British Government and was completely removed on cessation of hostilities. The severe gradient of the 1:20 branch meant that it was exclusively worked by CALEDONIA.

THE ADVENT OF THE MOTOR BUS

The tourist trade picked up again after the First World War but the railway found itself in competition with the motor coach. The railway had not suffered much from the horse drawn wagonettes and landaus but when the coach operators introduced motor driven coaches and charabancs, the competition was taken more seriously. Motor bus operations had been introduced within the Borough of Douglas by the Corporation in 1914 with a 25 seat Straker Squire omnibus. After the War, they expanded their fleet with a number of Tilling Stevens petrol-electric omnibuses.

The first serious bus service outside of Douglas was introduced in 1927 in the form of Manxland Bus Services Ltd. which had a strong connection with Cumberland Motor Services Ltd. The rural roads of the Island were by this time being greatly improved and surfaced with tar and chippings. Concerned at this potential competitor operating fourteen ADC 28 seat buses, the Isle of Man Railway Company took an interest in forming a consortium with other local operators and Manx Motors Ltd. was formed operating with eight Thornycroft buses.

The railway responded to this threat by operating 100 trains a day. It now had sixteen locomotives available, although in reality was only operating fourteen in regular service. The railway company had acquired their last and largest Beyer Peacock locomotive in 1926. Still in 2-4-0 format and named MANNIN it was built specially for the Port Erin line and was designed as a more powerful engine to reduce the need for banking or double heading on the climb out of Douglas through the Nunnery cutting or on the bank out of Ballasalla on the return journey. At present it can be seen as a static exhibit in the Railway Museum at Port Erin railway station.

The Manxland venture eventually went into liquidation, having made the mistake of under estimating the seasonal nature of the Island traffic. In the meantime, the railway company had formed yet another company, Isle of Man Road Services Ltd., operating the fastest vehicles which were 28 seat Thornycroft BC omnibuses. The Isle of Man Railway Company, operating its train service to capacity at cut price fares and also a faster more efficient bus service, eventually saw off the other bus competitors by 1930. This monopoly eventually was to work to the detriment of the railway but up to the outbreak of the Second World War was to guarantee a period of stability and consolidation of the Railway Company interests.

The Second World War was to see many changes in the Island and perhaps it is a good point at which to stop and consider the other rail systems that were built in the latter part of the nineteenth century, many of which exist to the present day.

THE TRAMWAYS

1870 was a significant year in the history of the development of Douglas and many decisions were taken which shaped the town as it exists today. Victoria Street was completed in 1875, having cut through much of old Douglas in the process. It joined a new promenade which was opened the same year by Governor Loch and still bears his name. The Loch Promenade was not completed until 1877 but it dramatically extended the sea wall some 300ft. seaward enabling the building of the grand façade of Victorian hotels and boarding houses, much of which remains to the present day.

Thomas Lightfoot, a retired civil engineering contractor, saw his opportunity with this new promenade and promoted his ideas for a horse tramway along the full length of Douglas Bay. By 1876 the Douglas Horse Tramway was partially completed and two trams were in operation carrying fare paying passengers. The line was completed in January 1877 and is still running. The 3ft. gauge tramway has been altered on a number of occasions to meet the development of the town but generally follows the original concept.

The tramway changed hands, eventually being purchased by the Isle of Man Tramways and Electric Power Company Ltd in 1894. The directors of this company, having seen the success of the horse tramway, were keen to extend their tramway operations to serve upper parts of the town, which was by this time being developed. Horse traction was not practical because of the steep gradients so they proposed to serve the town with a cable tramway.

By August 1896 the 1½ mile tramway had been laid from the Salisbury Hotel up Victoria Street, Prospect Hill, Bucks Road, Woodbourne Road, York Road and Broadway. A winding house and car shed was built at York Road to accommodate 15 cars.

Staker Squire single deck bus - the first bus operated by Douglas Corporation

Contractors laying the cable tramway in Victoria Street, Douglas in 1896

A full day was taken to thread the cable, using two traction engines, and the two ends were joined in an 80ft splice.

In 1902 the horse tramway and the cable tramway were purchased by the Douglas Corporation. The tramways ran as a municipal undertaking being supplemented by buses in 1914. By 1920 buses were operating on the Upper Douglas routes and by 1929 the cable cars were withdrawn and the York Road depot became the bus garage and workshops.

Sadly nothing remains of the cable tramway, the depot being demolished in 1989 to make way for housing development. Some diverter pulleys remain buried under the roadway and emerge from time to time during roadworks. Two cars, Nos.72 and 73, survived as a summer bungalow at the Lhen in the north of the island complete with their bogies but each with one side dismantled. Sufficient parts were salvaged to restore one complete car, which now forms an exhibit at the horse tramway depot at Strathallan Crescent.

In 1891 a scheme was promoted to build a marine drive from Douglas to Port Soderick. The company formed to undertake this ambitious project suffered financial and other set backs but by persistence the scheme developed and eventually incorporated a tramway.

Douglas Southern Electric Tramways was incorporated as a limited company in 1895. By 1896 a 4ft. 8½ ins. gauge line (the only standard gauge line in the Island) had been laid, including three major bridges and several half bridges replacing earlier timber viaducts. A generating station was built at Pigeon Stream to provide electric power at 550 volts d.c. for the twelve double-deck cars originally supplied, although only six were motor cars.

The crimson and white livery must have presented a pretty sight on the Marine Drive. Four additional trailer cars were provided by Brush Electrical Engineering Company in 1897 and two of these were later converted to motor cars at the tramway workshops at Little Ness.

Nothing remains of the tramway which closed in 1939 except the toll gate house and the odd metal sleeper incorporated in the roadside fence. The sites of various points of

MER No.6 tunnel car at Ballure crossing

interest are described in the walk which embraces the Marine Drive. The depot trackwork was removed to Crich Tramway Museum in 1960 and car No.1 remains preserved there.

Development is nothing new and today's development of the Isle of Man pales into insignificance against the background of the speculative ventures of the last quarter of the nineteenth century. The Howstrake Estate was being developed to provide housing on the grand scale and to open up access to this land roads had to be built.

The Douglas Bay Estate Ltd. with several shareholders and directors common to the Douglas Horse Tramway in 1882 started work on building a new coast road from Derby Castle towards Groudle. By 1893 Port e Vada creek had been filled in and a single line tramway of 3ft. gauge was built as far as Groudle Glen, where a new hotel was built. An electricity generating station and car sheds were built at Port e Vada and the depot occupies the same site today.

In the same year, the Douglas and Laxey Coast Electric Tramway Company was formed and soon acquired the Howstrake Tramway. By July 1894 trams were running to Laxey. The company acquired the Douglas Horse Tramway in 1894 and changed its name to Isle of Man Tramways and Electric Power Company Limited and also embarked on a policy of selling electric power as a side line.

It was to be 1899 before the tramway reached Ramsey with its double track on the same alignment that exists to the present time. Additional depots were built at Laxey and Ramsey. A further power station was built at Laxey and a final power station completed in 1898 at Ballaglass 12½ miles from Douglas. Most of the original rolling stock is still in use, except those damaged and destroyed in a fire at the Laxey depot in 1930.

The tramways of the Island had been financed by underwritings from Dumbell's Bank. There was a financial involvement with the directors of the Bank and the tramways which led to the collapse of the Bank. The tramway was rescued from receivership in 1902 by a new company, the Manx Electric Railway Company Limited.

In 1895 a 3ft 6ins gauge tramway was built from Laxey to the top of Snaefell, the highest point on the Island. The tramway was almost 5 miles long and had its own power station situated almost half way between Laxey and the summit. The Manx Northern Railway locomotive CALEDONIA was hired to haul the necessary construction trains during the laying of the track, running on a temporary third rail laid to the three feet gauge. As part of the celebrations for the centenary of the Snaefell Mountain Railway a temporary third rail was once again laid between The Bungalow and the Summit to allow CALEDONIA to run special trains to the summit.

After a period of use during the Second World War CALEDONIA had lain languishing in the running sheds at Douglas, having been used only occasionally for snow clearing duties. It survived a period of decline in the 1970s and ended in the Steam railway Museum at Port Erin. It was restored to full running order for the celebrations, propelling special trains to the summit during the year, after which it was returned to the running sheds at Douglas and can still be seen in steam for special events.

The original rolling stock of six cars, built for the SMR by Milnes of Salop, still exist and are housed in the original depot at Laxey. One of the cars, No.5, was recently re-built following a fire whilst in service.

The cars collect current from the overhead supply by Hopkinson rigid bow collectors. The centre rail is purely to guide the tram bogies and was originally used for braking on the descent using a form of calliper brake operated by the brakesman. These brakes are still retained for use in an emergency as since 1977 all the cars have been converted to rheostatic braking, using second hand equipment from a number of German tramcars purchased from Aachen. Traction is by adhesion and the average gradient of the line is 1 in 12.

1930 had been a disastrous year for the tram company, not only had the fire at Laxey destroyed four power cars and seven trailers but a flood later in the year had involved the Laxey power station, damaging its own installation and also contributing to additional damage in the lower part of the village, for which the company was held liable.

Although the advent of the Second World War in 1939 stopped the holiday traffic overnight there was to be an unexpected bonus for the Isle of Man Railway moving internees who were billeted in camps into requisitioned boarding houses in all of the Island's towns. There was also a corresponding movement of troops and in addition material from the Foxdale mines spoil heaps was moved to provide infill material for wartime airfields.

The Manx Electric Railway was less fortunate picking up little wartime trade, although mines spoil was also taken from Laxey to Ramsey as hardcore for constructing runways at the wartime airfields being built at Jurby and Andreas.

After the war ceased in 1945 the Island enjoyed a post war boom in the holiday trade but it was short lived and by 1950 it started to decline. The Manx Electric Railway, still smarting from the pre-war problems and suffering from lack of maintenance, came near to liquidation but finally was rescued by the Isle of Man Government in 1957.

The Isle of Man Railway was not so fortunate. Losses, coupled with bus competition from its own subsidiary company and the advent of the ubiquitous motor car, led to winter closures in the early 1960s on the Peel and Ramsey lines. With only eight locomotives available for work, maintenance of service became a problem. The end was in sight and 1966 appeared to be the point at which the company would go into liquidation and train operation did cease.

There was a slight reprieve when the railway was operated by a private consortium aided by a tourism grant. Eventually this was to fail and rails were removed from the

Foxdale, Peel and Ramsey lines. During this demolition work sparks from oxy-acetylene burners accidentally set fire to the carriage sheds at St. Johns and many irreplaceable coaches were destroyed. Fortunately, the Isle of Man Government stepped in and purchased the remaining railway lands and the Port Erin line, which had been protected by a lease, survived and steam trains continue to run on this line to the present day.

The Manx Electric Railway, Snaefell Mountain Railway and the Steam Railway are all operated by the Transport Division of the Department of Tourism and Transport, as is the fleet of modern buses.

The remains of a number of cliff lifts can still be seen around the Island and their location will be described in the walks.

The Falcon Cliff incline railway was built in 1887 and was originally a twin track with two cars linking the Falcon Cliff Hotel to the Douglas Promenade. This incline railway was removed in 1896 and re-erected one year later at Port Soderick to link the resort to the terminus of the Marine Drive Tramway. The site of the incline is still visible, as are some of the timber supports and features in Walk No.8. In 1927 a new cliff lift was built at Falcon Cliff to a 5 ft. gauge by the Wadsworth Lift Company and still survives, although not at present working.

The Douglas end of the Marine Drive Tramway was served by the Douglas Head Incline Railway from the Battery Pier. A double track funicular with two cars by Hurst Nelson and Company, the cable being operated by an oil engine situated at the head of the incline. It was demolished in the mid-1950s but its route can still be easily seen.

The Browside tramway was another two car funicular serving Laxey Wheel as a tourist attraction. It was built about 1890 but lasted barely twenty years. It was unusual in that water ballast was used to provide the operating power. There are very little remains to show where it was located.

The remains of one other very unusual cliff lift can be seen at Little Switzerland. A travolator was installed in the 1920s to assist campers returning to Cunningham's Holiday Camp from the shore. The camp was built on the cliff top behind Queens Promenade and the entrance at Little Switzerland was through a stone portico and up an enclosed timber clad tunnel which housed a set of steps for the energetic and a continuous chain to which chairs were fixed. The chairs faced outward and ran on a smooth track forming an escalator. It can still be seen but is in a state of dereliction.

CONTRACTORS TRAMWAYS

A number of contractors' tramways were built in the Island in connection with major civil engineering works and although well documented there are no remains other than bits of track formation here and there.

The most interesting without doubt was the Port Erin Harbour Tramway. The Isle of Man Harbour Commissioners engaged Sir John Coode, an eminent civil engineer, to design a breakwater to create a harbour of refuge at Port Erin to provide shelter from westerly gales.

Work commenced in 1864 and the Commissioners acquired a second-hand locomotive, three steam cranes and a number of wagons, all to a gauge of 7 ft. The 0-4-0 locomotive was the first steam locomotive to appear on the Island. Built in 1853 by Wilson and Company of Leeds, it is generally accepted that it had previously worked at Portland on harbour works.

The Harbour Commissioners named the engine HENRY B LOCH, whilst it was in their possession, after Governor Loch who was responsible for many of the development schemes occurring in the latter half of the nineteenth century. The tramway served the block making yard, a quarry and the breakwater. The site of the quarry is readily seen behind the former marine biological station. The workshops and engine shed still exist as a workshop and stores on the elevated area behind the lifeboat house which was part of the site of the block-making yard. The wide arched doorways to the sheds are the only remaining clue to the existence of the 7 ft. gauge tramway (See Walk No.7).

The breakwater was completed in 1876 but this grand structure was severely damaged during an inshore gale in 1881 and was finally demolished by the sea in 1884, ending up much as it is today.

In 1899 the Douglas Corporation commenced work on the construction of a new reservoir at Injebreck at West Baldwin. A tramway was built for the West Baldwin River Reservoir to a gauge of 3ft., eventually reaching a length of five miles. The ruling gradient was 1 in 58 and there were a number of timber bridges on the line. Traces of the track bed can be seen alongside the River Glass from the West Baldwin Road. The tramway linked the dam and claypit site to a number of quarries.

The first locomotive was acquired second-hand in 1899 and was a 0-4-0 saddle tank engine built by Andrew Barclay Sons and Company Limited. The loco was named INJEBRECK. The Corporation purchased two new Hunslet tank engines from Leeds in 1901. The first to arrive was a 0-6-0 which was named WEST BALDWIN and the second, which arrived two months later, was a 0-4-0 and was named ARDWHALLIN. A fourth loco was acquired in 1903, towards the end of the contract, second-hand from Hunslett and was another 0-4-0 named HANNAH. It was never re-named by the Corporation.

The furthermost point to which the line reached was a quarry at Cronk ny Mona near Hillberry and this extension was built in 1904, a reversing line, or switchback being incorporated to overcome the difference in height. The whole tramway was dismantled and sold after the completion of the dam in 1905 and the locomotives saw work on other contracts in the North of England.

At Poortown Quarry near Peel, the Island's Highways Committee operated a quarry to provide crushed granite road stone for parish foremen transported by means of the Manx Northern and later the Isle of Man Railway. A 2 ft. gauge tramway ran from the quarry to Poortown Halt along the side of the road on a falling gradient. Jubilee trucks loaded with stone descended by gravity to a loading bay above a short siding north of the road bridge. The empty trucks were brought back to the quarry by a horse, which was stabled at the quarry behind the compressor house. The line of the tramway has recently been obliterated by a new footpath but it is possible to see where it curved onto the loading bay which is still in place. The quarry has been modernised several times since 1923 when a steam driven compressor and crusher were installed and now is the principal stone quarry on the Island, producing 70,000 tons of stone per year.

The Abbey Clay Works near St. John's had a tramway connecting the Clay Pit at Ballaharra to the works which produced tiles and the tramway ran on top of an embankment which can still be seen opposite a sand pit still in use on the site of the old clay pit.

Many of the Island's quarries used the universal 2 ft. gauge track and trucks and the layout of the track changed to suit the workings. They were in fact the forerunner of the mechanical loader and reference is made to some of the locations in the description of the walks where appropriate.

A miniature railway was constructed in Groudle Glen as a visitor attraction and it has been restored to full working order by a group of local enthusiasts. A description of it is contained in walk No.6.

MINING

Whilst all of the walks are planned around these public transport systems, many embrace areas where traces of the Island's industrial past can be seen. Mining was perhaps the most lucrative of these industries and the earliest record of mining in the Island dates from 1246. The early history of mining for metalliferous ore is intertwined with the history of the Lords of Mann and beyond the scope of this book.

The principal search was for ore containing lead and copper, later silver, zinc blende and hematite and all were won in quantity. Moving the ore within the mines and their immediate surroundings involved tramways of varying sorts. Very little remains to be seen today other than at Laxey.

The earliest seems to have been wooden tram roads on which skids or wheeled buckets were pushed by the miners. Traces of wooden ways have been found in the oldest mine workings at Bradda near Port Erin, which were probably in use in the middle of the nineteenth century as by 1903 work in the North Bradda Mine had almost ceased. There is no doubt that some form of timber ways were used in the Foxdale mines to move the ore from the working face to the shafts but no documented evidence can be reliably quoted.

It is to the Laxey mines that we turn for the most extensive tramway and because they worked until 1929 it is well documented. The first reference to mining in Laxey dates from 1781 but it was to be 1845 before extensive investment took place leading to the formation in 1854 of the Great Laxey Mining Company, by which time the mines had reached a depth of 200 fathoms.

The Great Laxey Wheel was built and commissioned the same year for the purpose of draining the mine workings. Ore was hauled from the workings in a bucket-like device known as a 'kibble' and discharged at adit level into wagons to be taken to the washing floors for processing. The main adit provided the principal means of communication between the shafts and the washing floors. Rails were laid in the adit tunnel and it is believed that the ore wagons were originally hauled to the washing floors using horses.

Much research into the history of the mines has been undertaken and dates are more accurately being fixed. It can be said that between 1870 and 1875 access along the adit was improved and a 2 ft. gauge railway was laid from the washing floors to serve the main shafts, with motive power being provided by two small steam locomotives. Their size and height was dictated by the tunnel and they were only 4ft.9ins. to the top of the chimney. The engines were 0-4-0 tank locomotives built by the Lewin Engine Company of Poole. They continued to work until the mine closed in 1929 and were eventually scrapped in 1935.

The ore trains normally comprised seven wagons which were loaded directly over the shafts on a timber platform whilst the locomotive negotiated the shaft head on a by-pass cut into the rock. The trains were assembled by hand shunting and then taken to the washing floors where the ore was discharged by gravity into storage bunkers.

Very little surface remains of the tramway can be seen but recent underground investigation has revealed the extent of the tramway, much of which remains intact. Replica locomotives have been built by a group of enthusiasts and the tramway is being re-laid on its original alignment from the washing floors towards the adit. The water wheel originally used at the Snaefell Mine is being reconstructed on the washing floors. As more is learnt about the mine and its working so the Mines Heritage Trail will become perhaps the most comprehensive of its type in the British Isles. Even with the work completed to date, it should not be missed.

Much of the industrial heritage of the Island centres around the extractive industries and in particular the metalliferous workings which in general had ceased working by 1900, although Foxdale continued to 1911 and Laxey to 1929.

The earliest records of mining seem to point to Bradda near Port Erin in the south of the Island where the great lode was exposed

Foxdale Mines in their heyday during the 19th century showing Beckwith's (Foxdale) and Bawden's shaft

for all to see but what we see now is a great scar above the remains of the buildings at the South Bradda Mine. Workings probably existed at Port Erin from 1246. Early in the nineteenth century the workings were intermittently worked but by the middle of the century the Bradda Mining Company was operating both the South Bradda Mine and the North Bradda Mine, producing between 1869 and 1874 364 tons of lead ore and 193 tons of copper ore.

Both mines still show the remains of old galleries and the newer workings and the surface remains of office buildings and engine houses for the pumps. North Bradda Mine was sunk to a depth of 72 fathoms from the adit level, which was a little above sea level. The large surface remains housed the pumping engine used to lift 200 gallons of sea water per minute from the workings. The working conditions must have been terrible.

The Foxdale lode was eventually worked underground over a distance of four miles and although records exist of mining near the surface in the late part of the eighteenth century, by the middle of the nineteenth century depths of almost 200 fathoms in hard rock had been reached.

The most westerly mine was Beckwith's Mine, of which a number of surface remains survive, including a rather drunken chimney stack. This mine produced 50,000 tons of lead ore which had a value approaching £750,000. The mine reached a depth of 185 fathoms but by 1880 appears to have been worked out, although almost the last work done was to connect the main adit to Cross's Mine.

Cross's Mine stands as a landmark on the saddle between South Barrule and Slieau Whallian and is known locally as "Snuff the Wind". The mine was productive in its upper levels but produced nothing at the lower levels. The two shafts were sunk to a depth of 80 fathoms. From Cross's Mine looking east about quarter of a mile are the remains of the surface buildings and the two shafts of Dixon's Mine. The engine shaft reached a depth of 47 fathoms and this mine too was more productive near the surface. By 1868 the mine had ceased working.

At Foxdale there was by far the greatest

activity, with a number of shafts being sunk at several locations and eventually all coming under the control of the Isle of Man Mining Company in 1828. Mining started in the early part of the eighteenth century with surface working of the exposed Foxdale Vein which continued in a west to east direction.

The three main shafts at Foxdale, of which some surface remains exist, start with the most westerly, which was Bawden's shaft, sunk to a depth of 260 fathoms by 1902, having been opened in 1855. Beckwith's shaft by the same date had reached 320 fathoms and was said to be hot in its lower levels. The third shaft was Potts which bottomed at 200 fathoms. There was a distance of 750 yards between the two extreme shafts although the length of the underground workings was 1,510 yards, with galleries and levels almost every 10 fathoms.

It is hard to comprehend now the extent of these workings and the buildings on the surface with numerous water wheels, steam engines and such. How were they transported to these comparatively remote areas at that time? Some of the answers are to be found in the Manx National Museum where documents and photographs exist. Where did all the people live? Over 300 men worked in the mines. If you examine some of the photographs carefully you would also see that women and children were employed.

If you go to Foxdale, sit up on the Shoulder Road near the entrance to South Barrule slate quarry and look over the district, pick out some of the features and let your mind drift back in time. While you do that just consider also that these mines in the latter half of the nineteenth century produced a total of 149,063 tons of lead ore all dug by hand, from which about 50 tons of silver was won. The mines in the area were driven through slate at the upper levels then ending in granite.

The vein continued in an easterly direction and at the Eairy the southern branch of the lode was worked by the Central Foxdale Mines in the latter part of the nineteenth century on the site of earlier workings. There were three shafts named Amy, Elizabeth and Taylors. Although one shaft was sunk to a depth of 145 fathoms and almost 5,000 tons of lead ore produced between 1872 and 1889, the mine did recoup its expenses but was closed by the turn of the century. The vein was chased further east by workings at Cornelly, described in one of the walks in greater detail, and finally at Ellerslie by the Glen Darragh Mine.

The Laxey vein ran in a north to south direction and although not as productive as Foxdale in respect of lead ore it had a high rate of output of zinc blende. The lead, however, produced silver of exceptional quality. The earliest records of mining at Laxey date from 1781, adits being driven from Glen Mooar following surface exposures. By 1822 the Lonan Mining Company had been established and under the direction of the mine's captain, Richard Rowe, extensive works were commenced to develop the area and deepen the two shafts, which were at this time 130 fathoms deep.

Washing floors were built lower down the valley and the crowning glory was the building of a wheel to pump the water from the mine which was completed in 1847. This was not the present wheel but it was designed by the same man, Robert Casement, the mines engineer, and it was at that time the largest wheel in the Island.

In 1848 the Laxey Mining Company was formed and they were employing almost as many men as the Foxdale mines. By 1854 the company name was changed yet again to the Great Laxey Mining Company and the same year the Great Laxey Wheel was commissioned with much pomp and circumstance. Lady Isabella Hope, the wife of Governor Hope, gave her name to the wheel which is still known as 'The Lady Isabella' and the 72½ft diameter wheel still stands as a tribute to the skill of the men who worked these mines.

The wheel was built to pump water from the mines which had reached a depth of 200 fathoms (a fathom is 6 ft., which in turn is 1.82 metres). Pumping was carried out by a series of pumps in the Engine shaft to which the wheel was connected by a rod duct of graceful stone arches carrying a rod on a series of rollers which converted the wheel's motion into a vertical reciprocating movement through a huge T rocker beam.

There are a number of similar T rockers located down the shaft to the 235 fathom level connected to the near vertical operating rod which operated the pumps and lifted water through a series of sumps to the main adit level, which has been described earlier. The water ran out along the tramway to discharge into the Laxey River. Go to Laxey Wheel and walk up to the Engine shaft, ponder the weights involved and imagine how those miners handled the heavy timbers and castings, lowered them down the shaft and assembled them underground with little or no light.

There were seven main shafts, the oldest being the Engine shaft which commenced in 1824 reaching a depth of 247 fathoms below adit level. The Welch shaft was sunk in 1829 reaching 295 fathoms. Dumbells shaft and Slide shaft were commenced in the early 1850s and eventually culminated in the main shaft known as Dumbells which reached a depth of 302 fathoms and was the deepest at Laxey. Corner shaft, Agneash shaft and North shaft were all commenced in the early part of the 1860s but never reached any significant depth.

The length of the underground galleries extends for a distance of 1¼ miles to end well up the valley under Agneash village. Levels were driven every 10 fathoms and all of the shafts were connected but not at every level. Most of the workings were dug in slate but dykes of granite were encountered throughout the mine.

There are many interesting surface remains at Laxey and the wheel is without doubt the most dominant and is world famous into the bargain. What is not so well known, but in many ways more interesting, is

Laxey washing floors with the Haymen water lift and showing the huge spoil heap

the Man engine situated below the surface in the Welch shaft. A 12 ft. stroke water pressure engine, installed in 1881, was connected to a man rod which descended the shaft to at least the 200 fathom level. The rod was made up from 10" x 7" baulks of timber connected by iron straps and supported by large iron rollers. The tremendous weight of the rod was counter-balanced by three T rockers and ballast boxes. Miners used the man engine to climb and descend the mine by stepping on and off iron platforms fixed to both sides of the rod every 12 ft. matching the stroke of the pressure engine, and corresponding with platforms on the side of the shaft. It took a miner twenty-five minutes to reach adit level from the 200 fathom level - almost twice as quick as the alternative which was to climb the ladders.

It is hard to imagine the working conditions where men had to climb down ladders 1,200 ft. (365 metres) do a day's work and then climb back up again and repeat it six days a week! The only light that the miners had to work with was a candle stuck in a lump of clay on his hat. It is almost beyond belief.

The Laxey vein was worked further up the valley under the shadow of Snaefell by the same company. The Great Snaefell Mine is described in more detail in Walk No.18, as is the North Laxey Mine which represents the northernmost extremity to which the Laxey vein was worked.

There are numerous small trials and mines scattered around the Island additional to these main areas and descriptions of some appear within the text of the walks.

In proportion to its size the mining wealth of the Isle of Man in the nineteenth century was outstanding. A total of 233,292 tons of lead ore, 215,397 tons of zinc ore and 150 tons of silver were recorded as having been produced between 1845 and 1900. Small amounts of copper and iron were also recorded.

QUARRIES

Before leaving the extractive industries, mention should be made of the various quarries around the Island. From the early part of the eighteenth century each parish had quarries from which slate building stone was taken. In 1713, Tynwald, the Island's government, introduced the first Highway Act, appointed an Overseer of Highways and placed an onus of repair on landowners. This, coupled with the Boundary Walls Act of 1713, increased the demand for stone.

The large quarries at Douglas, Ramsey and Peel provided building stone for the developing towns. Quarries were opened at Peel and South Barrule for roofing slate with some of the largest workings at Glen Rushen and Sulby Glen where levels and inclines can still be seen. Despite a great deal of expense in opening these quarries in search of good slate none was found suitable for export as had been the case in Wales. Most of the activity seems to have been in the latter half of the nineteenth century and although inferior roofing slates and building stone were sold on the Island, the quarries were largely unprofitable.

At Glen Rushen, where the levels and tips can still be clearly seen on the south flank of the valley, 120 men were recorded as working in these quarries in 1863. South Barrule Quarry had 45 men working and produced slate for local use. An interesting relic from that period still remains in the form of a wind-driven saw with cut marks from the saw still visible on the slate bench. The quarry is still used today for the production of building stone but remains uneconomic to operate.

95 men were employed in the slate quarry in Sulby Glen near the site of the present Block Eary Reservoir where extensive surface remains of the quarrying can be seen. By 1880 all of these quarries had ceased work. Only South Barrule and a smaller quarry at Cronk Fedjag have continued at various times since that date.

Great Mona Mine at Ballaglass

Stone for road-making purposes was eventually centred on six main quarries at Glenduff, Dhoon, Oatland, Ellerslie, Poortown and Cregneash. The first two mentioned used a system of aerial ropeways for moving stone and had faces worked into a hillside. Oatland went down below ground level and had a main floor at 80ft and a lower floor at 120ft. which flooded. It was served by a rope incline but is now completely obliterated by landfill. Only Poortown remains in production, as mentioned earlier.

Limestone has always been quarried in the south of the Island with some very old workings and lime kilns at Ballahot and Ballasalla. Quarries are still worked at Balladoole, Turkeyland and Billown for road and building purposes. Much of Castletown (including the Castle) was built from limestone and there are disused quarries at Scarlett from where most of that stone was won.

A number of clay pits were dug at various times and bricks produced. The two most significant sites were at Ballacorey, Andreas, where a bright red brick was produced from boulder clay, and at Glenfaba, where slatey clay produced many thousands of common bricks which were burnt at Peel near the site of the present Power Station, the operation only ceasing within the last three decades, when the production of concrete bricks hastened the demise of the traditional clay brick. The brick works did at one time have a horse tramway connecting the kilns to the large quarry on the side of Peel Hill. It fell into disuse when better quality clay was won from a quarry at Glenfaba and hauled to site by road.

So now to the walks which are divided into four sections to appeal to walkers of all ages and abilities. They utilise public transport to access the start and finish points and embrace much of the industrial heritage described in the introduction.

WALK I
DOUGLAS

The first walk is a town trail exploring Douglas and is approximately 5km long and will take 2hrs.

Starting in front of the Sea Terminal forecourt, it is worth taking time to look at this building which was completed in 1962. The circular part of the structure immediately below the spire, although now offices, was originally a restaurant. It commanded views of the bay and harbour unrivalled anywhere on the Island. The unusual roof to this part of the terminal earned it the nickname of the 'lemon squeezer'. The building was formally opened by Princess Margaret in 1965.

Walk around the front of the building towards the Imperial Buildings, which is the office of the Isle of Man Steam Packet Company. Cross the entrance to the harbour marshalling area and follow the footpath around the corner to the inner harbour, keeping to the left-hand side of Bath Place. Notice the unusual roundabout at the junction surmounted by two cannons and in front of the police station!

You are heading for the Millennium Bridge which was opened in 2001, replacing an earlier swing bridge. The accumulator tower and control room for the old bridge can still be seen on the other side of the harbour.

Cross the road at the bridge, with care, to the harbour side and read the inscriptions on the plaques which have been fixed to blocks of Foxdale granite. The inner harbour was until recently a commercial harbour and was tidal. At the time that the new bridge was installed a tidal flap was built and the enclosed basin became a yacht marina, part of an ongoing overall plan to redevelop the harbour as a focal point for Douglas.

Walk along the harbour behind the parked cars and cross the road opposite the old Fish Market, now the Royal British Legion Club, and continue along the North Quay. The Market and the British Hotel are the next buildings that are passed. The harbour frontage is gradually changing but much of its past can still be traced on this part of the quay.

At the junction of North Quay and Ridgeway Street is St. Matthews Church dating from 1895, which was built at a time when the old heart of Douglas was being redeveloped and when new streets were being driven through the town, which had by this time become the capital of the Island.

Continue along North Quay and look for the plaque on the building on the right, just before arriving at Queen Street. You will see that the building was in fact the first electricity generating station for the town, having been opened in 1922. At the junction with Queen Street perhaps the last vestige of the old character of the area can just be imagined. Directly opposite is a building forming part of the Newson Trading block, which was formerly the Liver Hotel. Opposite is the Saddle Hotel at the mouth of

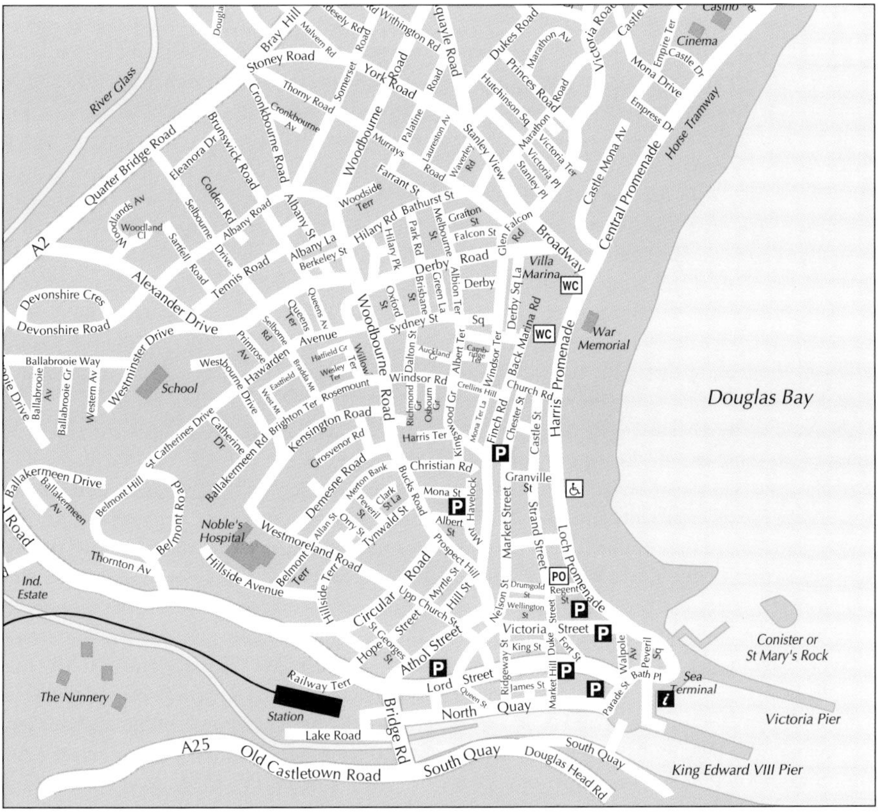

the old narrow alignment of Queen Street winding round the rear of the quay to Quines Corner completing the picture.

The area had many more public houses than now and earned it the reputation of the 'Barberry Coast'. As you walk along the quay to the top of the harbour you will see that the old and the new have blended together to keep some of the character of the old harbour frontage. The Bridge Inn remains as it was and on the corner of Bank Hill the outline of Clinches Brewery can still be seen incorporated in the modern development.

Cross Bank Hill and walk into the Railway Station forecourt through the elaborate entrance. Part of the old railway company offices are now occupied as the Custom House. This is where you will take the train on some of the walks in the south of the Island so it is worth looking inside the booking hall to get your bearings.

From the forecourt climb the steps leading to the clock tower and upper entrance. At the top of the steps pause and look back at the grand building in red facing brick, built at the start of the 20th century at the time that the Isle of Man Railway Company acquired the other two railway operating companies. The station was the envy of many mainland railway operators.

Go through the entrance gates and cross into Athol Street by crossing the top of Bank Hill and then, using the traffic lights, cross to Athol Street and walk along the street on the right-hand side. By the start of the 19th century it represented the upper limits of Douglas, the Georgian styled houses being the residences of merchants and the wealthy. As the town expanded it quickly became the business centre of the town, which it still is. Much of the street has been redeveloped but here and there you can still see some of the original buildings.

Walk as far as the junction with Lower Church Street and turn right and walk down the hill past the new multi-storey car park. At the bottom of the hill you will join John Street. The building on the corner on the left is probably the oldest surviving building of old Douglas, dating from about 1750. Opposite is the John Street elevation of the Town Hall and the site of the original fire station for the town.

Continue down Lower Church Street as far as its junction with Lord Street. On the right is the Salvation Army Citadel. The present building was opened in 1932. The Salvation Army had occupied two premises in Douglas before that time. The Salvation Army came to the Island on 21st June 1883 and Staff Captain Haddon was present for the opening ceremony at premises in Circular Road, which then was on the periphery of Douglas. This was only eighteen years after William Booth founded the East London Revival Society and five years after it was reorganised as the Salvation Army. Continually adapting to the changing needs of society, a major refurbishment of the Lord Street Citadel was undertaken in 1981. Now the building houses a playschool, a centre for the elderly, clubs for the young and provides a place for regular Sunday worship.

Turn left and walk back to the roundabout with the cannon. Now turn left along Walpole Avenue to join the Promenade opposite the Jubilee Clock, turn left and join Victoria Street. You are now at the lower terminus of the Upper Douglas Cable Tramway; a small section of track is laid in the pedestrian area but it is not original.

The walk continues along Victoria Street, following the route of the former cable tramway which had twin tracks. One of the first buildings you pass on the left is the former Salisbury Hotel. Look at the ornate filigree work in the tympanum above the entrance. The chariot in full flight is carrying the Greek God Helios driving the sun across the sky because as originally built the building was the Sun Hotel! It was at the time one of the principal hotels of the town and its speciality was 22 year old brown brandy.

At the head of Victoria Street continue up

Prospect Hill passing several of the national banks. Pay particular attention to the National Westminster Bank, which was originally Dumbell's Banking Company Limited. Its directors were key players in the tramway and mining interests in the Island which led to its collapse in 1900 with disastrous consequences for many residents of the town.

On reaching Athol Street observe the Italianate styled Isle of Man Bank headquarters. The other side of Prospect Hill has been re-developed with new office buildings presenting a stark contrast in styles.

Continue up Prospect Hill as far Hill Street and pause before turning left to look at the 'wedding cake corner' now being completely restored and expanded and forming part of the administrative buildings of the Isle of Man Government and the Parliament buildings. On the opposite corner of Hill Street is St Mary's Roman Catholic Church, designed by Henry Clutton and opened in 1859.

Leave the route of the tramway and walk along Hill Street. You will note more new office development reflecting the new found wealth of the town. At the end of Hill Street turn right into Upper Church Street and opposite is St George's Church, from which the street gets its name. It is worth going inside the church gates to look at the tomb of Sir William Hillary, founder of the Royal National Lifeboat Institution.

Walk up as far as Circular Road and turn right, crossing over to walk on the left-hand side of the road to its junction with Prospect Hill again. Opposite, at the other end of Government Buildings, are the Rolls Office and the new Court House. Now turn left and continue up Bucks Road, once the main route out of Douglas to the north and also the route of the cable tramway.

Carry on as far as Rosemount, pausing to admire the fine spire of Trinity Methodist Church. Continue straight on past Prospect Terrace and the shops which were originally built as private houses, the extent of the

T.E.Brown - the Island's celebrated poet

original terrace being framed by the pediments. The cable tramway had hitherto run in the centre of the roadway but at Prospect Terrace and into Woodbourne Road the tracks diverged to run alongside the kerb of the pavements on each side.

At the junction with Hawarden Avenue is Woodbourne Square, laid out in the late 19th century and one of several which retain the Victorian character of the town. Walk into the square enter the gardens and walk to the left around the perimeter of the square. Pause half way along the next side and look at the four corners of the square laid out with planting of palm and monkey puzzle trees – the Kew Gardens of Douglas!

Go out the opposite gate and cross straight over the road and leave the Square, turning left again into the Woodbourne Road - which you should cross with care. You now leave the route of the tramway which continued for a further three quarters of a mile to the depot and winding house. In 1896 there was very little development beyond this point. The cable tramway continued from the depot down York Road into Broadway as a single track and had a second terminal at the Villa Marina on the promenade.

There were track connections with the horse tramway at Broadway and Victoria Street to enable horsecars to be maintained and painted at York Road depot, being coupled to a cable car for the passage over the cable tramway rails. This practice continued long after the cable tramway was removed with horsecars being towed to York Road up Broadway on a trailer behind a bus!

The building that is on your left is now the Masonic Lodge. When the tramway was built it was Woodbourne House and the original building can still be seen incorporated into the rest of the structure. Follow the pavement around towards the Hilary Park, the next town square which you will visit. The Park is totally different to the square you have just seen. Stop to pause for thought at the modest memorial erected in 1995 marking the fiftieth anniversary of the cessation of hostilities in the Second World War.

Leave the Park opposite the terrace of yellow brick houses and turn right, walking as far as Derby Road where you must turn left. Walk downhill and look for the right turn into Derby Square opposite the Bowling Green Hotel. Here is yet another Victorian Square to explore. Walk in the gate on the corner and turn immediately left and follow the path down to admire the bronze by Manx sculptor F M Taubman. Then walk diagonally through the park and leave by the opposite corner on Derby Square.

Continue along to the top of Crellins Hill. Opposite is the Manx National Museum, the older part of which was originally the town hospital. Walk down the steep hill to St Thomas Church, which took three years to build and was completed in 1849. It was dedicated to St Thomas, the patron Saint of Architecture, and was designed by Ewan Christian RIBA, an architect of Manx descent who was Architect to the Church Commissioners (1814 - 1895) and noted particularly for his work at Carlisle Cathedral. The building work was undertaken by local contractor Richard Cowle. It was built to serve the needs of an expanding town and the arrival of the tourist development along Loch Promenade led to it being referred to as 'the visitor's church'.

It has a beautiful Venetian glass mosaic in the chancel floor and interesting murals by J M Nicholson which have been recently restored. A fire in the tower in 1912 destroyed the bells and the organ that had been built and installed in 1886 by William Hill of London. The fire damage was repaired and a new peal of bells replaced five months later. At the same time the organ was repaired and enlarged, providing the Island with what is considered to be the finest instrument in the Island. So much so that recitals and concerts are a regular feature of church life.

The school adjacent to the church dates from 1876 and remains the only Church of England Primary School in the Island. It was designed free of charge by the local monumental mason Charles Swinnerton.

Keep to the left-hand pavement, cross the road and walk down Church Road Marina to the promenade. Turn left, walking past the Sefton Hotel to the Gaiety Theatre. If the theatre is open for conducted tours it is worth finishing your walk with a tour of this beautiful gem, one of the few remaining examples of theatres designed by Frank Matcham. Otherwise, cross the promenade at the nearby pedestrian crossing to the promenade walkway, pausing to look back at the theatre and the newly-refurbished Villa Marina.

Return to the Sea Terminal along the promenade or by way of the sunken gardens and admire the Victorian façade of the Loch Promenade displaying the last of the fine boarding houses that graced more or less the whole of the bay.

WALK 2
CASTLETOWN

Travel to Castletown by the Steam Railway or take a No.1 or No.2 bus for this walk around the former capital of the Island which starts at the Railway Station. This will give you the ideal opportunity to arrive at Castletown by train and sample the delights of Victorian travel for a leisurely stroll around the town.

From the station, cross the railway lines and walk into Poulsom Park and walk across the park adjacent to the children's play area to emerge through a gate directly opposite on the bank of the Silverburn River. Turn left and walk beside the river.

Pass under the railway bridge where you will almost certainly be accosted by the resident population of geese and ducks. Walk up to Alexander Road and cross the road to join Victoria Road, continuing beside the Silverburn River. There straight ahead is the imposing grey bulk of Castle Rushen, around which the town grew to become the ancient capital of the Island.

The Castle beckons, but first a detour. Cross the road at School Lane and walk past Victoria Road Primary School, passing the unusually named Smetana Close, so named because of the close association the town has with many continental musicians through a music festival held annually in the town.

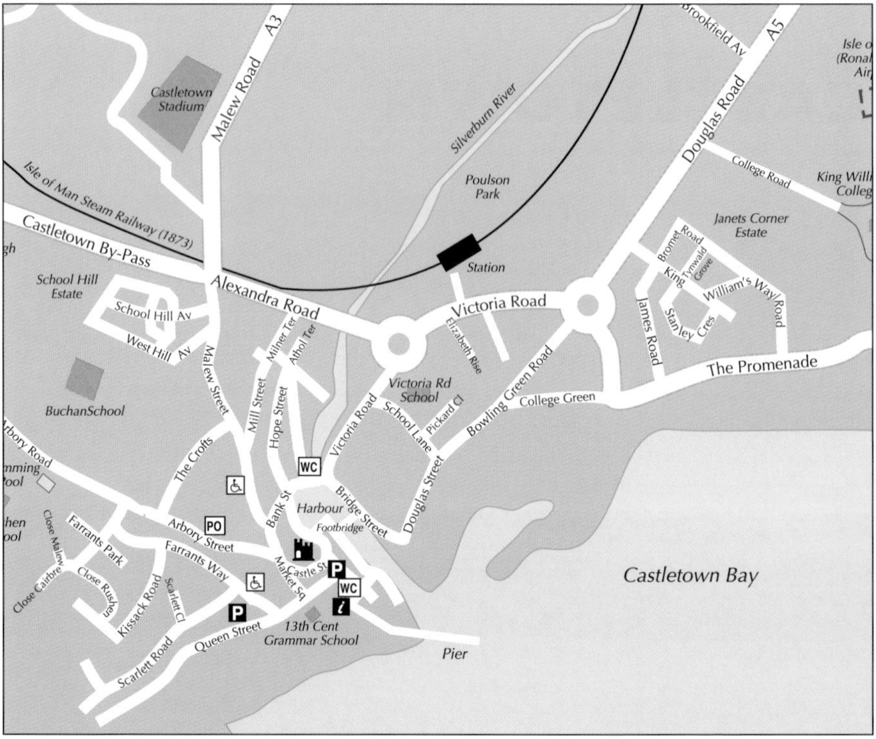

Emerge past the gates of Lorne House, which was a former residence of the Governors of the Island, onto Douglas Street and turn right. If you can't see Lorne House from here you will be able to find it from the top of the keep in the castle. Look out across Castletown Bay at the long peninsula of Langness with the prominent Lighthouse at its southernmost tip. Walk along the pavement to the corner with Bridge Street and past the Nautical Museum, part of the Story of Mann, presenting a history of the fishing industry of the Island and also housing the *Peggy*, the oldest surviving Manx-built ship. Continue as far as Bridge House, once the home of the Quayle family. To find out more visit the Nautical Museum.

On joining the harbour, turn left and cross the harbour, over the swing bridge and there is the castle in all its glory. Straight ahead on the corner is the local Police Station, designed so sympathetically to the castle by Baillie Scott. Across the road is the castle barbican, the entrance to the castle which you should make a point of visiting. The castle is one of the best preserved medieval castles in the British Isles, largely because it is built of limestone and has remained in use throughout most of its life. Its history is very much part of the history of the Island. The site is known to have been used by the Norse Kings of Mann to defend the fertile southern plain.

Turn left and walk along the quay a short distance before turning right up the narrow Quay Lane leading into what is now a public car park. Ahead is the old Grammar School, almost certainly the oldest intact building in the Island. It incorporates part of the medieval chapel of St Mary within its structure, dating from 1698 and pre-dating most of the castle buildings. It too is part of the Story of Mann and you can learn more about the town from the presentation on the walls and get a feel for what school was like in the nineteenth century.

Turn immediately right and walk into Parliament Square, which forms the forecourt to the old House of Keys building where the Island's Parliament met from 1706 until Douglas became the capital of the Island. After many varied uses it has become part of the Story of Mann and should be included in your list of places to visit.

Turn left into Castle Street and walk into the Parade and cross the road to pause and admire the best view of the Castle and its unique one-fingered clock presented to the Island by Queen Elizabeth I in 1597. The Castle as it stands now dates from the latter part of the 16th century but parts of it were built as early as 1250AD. The dominant feature of the castle is its massive keep with its four flanking towers.

If you look to the right, at the other end of the Parade is Market Square, which has as its backdrop the former garrison church of St Mary's, dating from 1826 when it replaced the old church, part of which is incorporated in the Old Grammar School. It is now de-consecrated and converted into offices and the façade has been preserved as part of the streetscape. In the centre of the Square there is a fine Doric column built to commemorate Colonel Cornelius Smelt, who was a much-respected Governor and who died in 1832. He was the last Governor to reside in the Castle, all subsequent Governors residing at Lorne House. Unfortunately the column never received his statue.

Continue along Arbory Street, which is the left-hand road of the two which leave the Parade. The shops in this street have changed little over the years and are much sought after by the newly-formed Island film industry as sets for many of the film-makers attracted to the island.

When reaching the Crofts, turn right and admire the part of the old capital where the wealthy of the day lived. Half way along the Crofts go in through the gate on the right to the municipal bowling green and walk past the café and green to emerge in Malew Street and turn left and then right to walk down Mill Street.

This area has recently been redeveloped under the guidance of the Local Commissioners to bring people back into the centre of the town. At the end of Mill Street turn right into Hope Street. Opposite is Qualtrough's yard, now a builders' merchant but in the past it was the site of a very active ship-building yard run by the same family. Walk back towards the centre of the town along Mill Street. At the end of the street is a limestone building, formerly the National School and now converted for use as a replacement for St Mary's Church.

You will have seen most of the eating establishments on this short walk through the town. Now is your chance for lunch before visiting the castle. If you are running out of time, then turn left and cross the bridge over the harbour to walk back along the harbour side to return to the starting place of the walk at the railway station.

Castletown harbour

WALK 3
PEEL

Take a No.5 or No.6 bus to Peel and get off at the House of Manannan. The walk around Peel starts outside the Creek Inn in Station Place. Directly opposite is the House of Manannan, which is part of The Story of Mann, and if not already visited is a must on completion of this short walk around the town. The Creek was formerly the Railway Hotel and you will have gathered by now that the Steam Railway did at one time reach Peel, and so it did. The old railway station is now incorporated into the House of Manannan and fronts onto the square.

The walk is another leisurely town stroll with ample time to visit the House of Manannan and the Castle. Start by heading away from the harbour and right into Mill Road. Passing the back of the House of Manannan, if you look carefully you will see that the goods shed of the railway has also been incorporated into the museum.

I suppose that this would have been and still is to some extent what we would now call the industrial heart of Peel, with the former town gas works on the left together with the kipper yards and the site of the old brickworks. Peel Heritage Trust has in fact established a small museum in the brickworks weighbridge office, which is worthy of a visit.

Opposite the weighbridge the station yard has now become a boat park, but the water tower of the railway, which crossed Mill Road as it left Peel, has been preserved.

Where Mill Road joins the harbour, Moore's kipper yard still preserves herring in the traditional manner and in season operates conducted tours of the establishment. Turn right here and walk alongside the harbour back towards the Creek. Peel is dominated by Peel Hill and Corrins Hill and worthy of a walk to the top.

Join East Quay after passing the impressive entrance to the House of Manannan. Continue along the quayside for a short distance, passing the remains of some of the warehousing which serviced the fishing industry, for so long the mainstay of Peel's economy and shortly to be developed into apartments to complement the water retention scheme recently completed.

At St. Peter's Lane turn right and walk up the narrow street, passing some grand stone-built houses originally occupied by those engaged in the fishing business. At the top of the hill turn left skirting the whitewashed wall which enclosed the churchyard of St. Peter's Church, which was built as a chapel of ease to the original St German's Cathedral on St Patrick's Isle. It was demolished in 1958 but the clock tower remains and the grounds are retained as a place of quiet reflection.

As you walk along the lane the architecture of the tower gives an indication of the style of the former church. Turn left into Castle Street and then right into Love Lane and then left into Market Street. Continue down the hill to the double corner, at the second corner look for the opening on the right. Walk through it into Charles Street, which is a charming part of old Peel. Many of the buildings in Peel are built of sandstone and here the beauty of the stone can be seen to advantage.

Continue through Charles Street and Strand Street into Beach Street and turn left

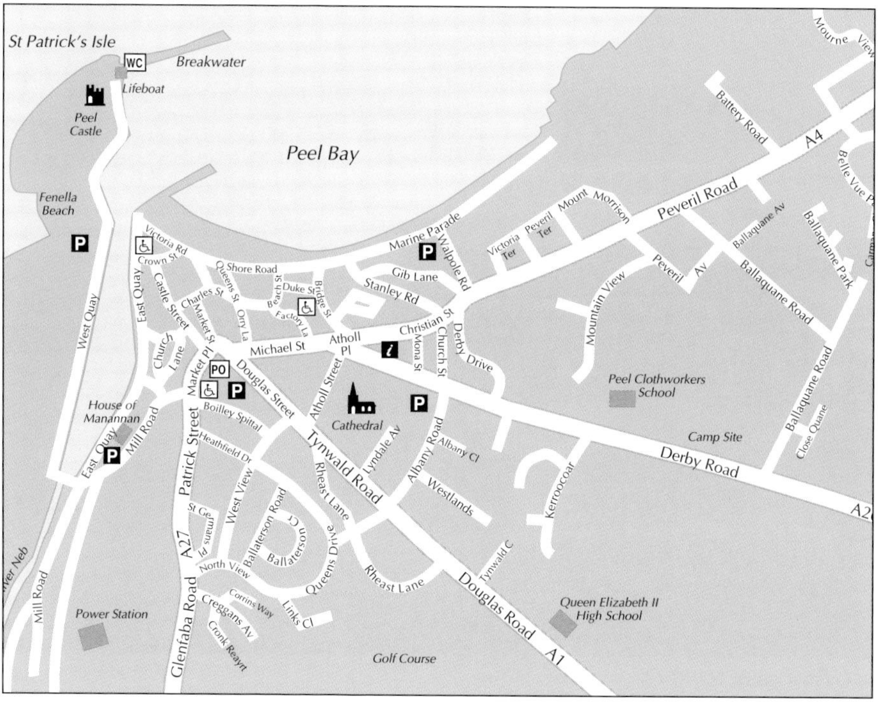

onto the promenade. Here you will pass some of the oldest former fishermen's cottages still remaining in the town. Turn right on the promenade, pausing to admire the Castle on St Patrick's Isle having its origins in a Norse settlement and that too, as mentioned earlier, is worth a visit.

Continue along the promenade as far as Stanley Road, turn right and half way up the hill turn right again into Circular Road. Walk up the hill to the corner at the top and cut through the alleyway into Christian Street, turning left and then right into Mona Street. Peel had many Methodist Churches, nearly all of which are no longer places of worship but their spirit remains in their architecture.

Walk up Mona Street to emerge almost opposite the Courthouse and Police Station. Cross Derby Road and enter the grounds of St German's Parish Church, now dedicated as the Island's new Cathedral. Although the church dates from 1884 and was built as the Parish Church it was only consecrated as the new Cathedral in 1980.

Walk down through the church grounds to emerge through the grand entrance gates into Athol Street opposite the Methodist Church. Turn right to Athol Place and turn left down Michael Street, which was the main shopping thoroughfare of the town but is now suffering the fate of many town centres. However, some businesses remain, giving a flavour of what it was once like.

At the end of the street turn right into Douglas Street and then left at Market Place. Now you can imagine the commanding position which St Peter's Church held, overlooking the old part of the town.

Cross the square and follow the church boundary wall to Lake Lane and walk down to Station Place and the completion of the walk.

Isle of Man Railway No. 3 Tender taking water at Peel

WALK 4
LAXEY

A 2km walk for which you should allow 1½ hours, being a short walk around Laxey with the Mines Heritage trail as its objective.

Take the Manx Electric Railway from Douglas, making sure that it is either the Ramsey or Laxey tram. Make sure that you ask the tram to stop at South Cape. Alight from the electric car (local people seldom refer to them as trams) and you will see the sign ahead announcing South Cape for Old Laxey and the beach.

Leaving the stop make your way to the road and follow it down towards the sea. At the junction turn right and then right again on Old Laxey Hill, which is quickly reached. Walk up the hill for a short way looking for footpath sign pointing left down to the promenade. It is a short but steep path and you will have a good view over the promenade and shore. Laxey beach is quite stony at high tide, but when the tide is out there is a pleasant stretch of sand, ideal for children to play.

Making your way along the promenade to the harbour, you will pass a large warehouse which was built originally by the Great Laxey Mining Company, as indeed was the harbour. Turn left and walk beside the harbour as far as the junction with Old Laxey Hill. Cross the road and walk through the car park of the Shore Hotel and follow the path on the left hand bank of the river. There are very little visible remains of the activity in this area.

The path follows the route of a proposed tramway which was never built but originally intended to carry coal from the harbour to the electricity generating station of the Douglas & Laxey Tramway Company. The first building that you come across was a turbine house. Commissioned in 1899 it housed two horizontal water-driven turbines which generated 160 amps at 520 volts and provided a cheap source of power for the electric tramway in the winter months.

Continuing past this building walk alongside the river before climbing to walk alongside the course of the water supply to the turbines which came from dams built into the river upstream. You can see one of the thrust blocks which carried the pipe down to the turbines. Now go back down again towards the river and the large building straight ahead. This was the Laxey Power Station built in 1894 by the parent company, the Isle of Man Tramways and Electric Power Company Limited. It housed two Galloway boilers providing steam for a pair of 90 hp engines driving two Mather and Platt dynamos producing 500 volts dc at 100 amps.

The cost of generating power on this section of tramway was very costly and in winter proved to be uneconomic, which was why the turbine house was built downstream. The station was modified in 1903 with additional boilers and new triple expansion 400 hp steam engines to produce 7,000 volts ac at 25 cycles and continued to operate until a disastrous flood in September 1930 almost crippled the company financially. In 1934 the company ceased generating its own power and bought in electricity from the public supply.

Cross the river by the bridge in front of the building and turn left into Glen Road. It is worth making a short detour almost opposite this point to view a small waterfall beside what is now a highway depot but which used to be a slaughter-house for the area.

Continue up the Glen Road, on the left the remnants of the old weir can be seen which dammed the river to provide water for the tramway generating station. It had a system of self-tipping weir flood-gates designed to operate in times of high water flow. It was their failure to work in September 1930 which caused the river to overflow down the Glen Road causing considerable damage for which the tramway company was eventually held responsible.

At the junction of the Glen Roy and Laxey River (the village getting its name from Lax, the Latin name for salmon) you are at the St George's Woollen Mills which were introduced by John Ruskin in 1881 in a former cornmill and where Manx tweed can still be seen woven on hand looms. Continue straight on at the Mills through Cooil Roi residential housing into what was the area occupied by the lower washing floors of the Laxey Mines. Although much modified, some of the features can still be seen.

On leaving the housing, look on the right for a flight of steps and follow them up to a path which will lead up to the site of an interesting railway which is in the process of restoration. The 19 inch tramway ran underground for most of its length, bringing the ore in wagons from the mine shafts to the washing floors which were built in 1847, as described in the introduction. Originally it is thought that the ore wagons were hauled by horse, the steam locomotives being introduced in 1875. The arch under the viaduct through which ore trains entered the washing floors is still in place.

The original locomotives were scrapped on cessation of the mine working but two replica locomotives have been built and track has been re-laid through the tunnel and to the upper washing floors, ending at present in the vicinity of the main adit. It is a novel experience to run through this tunnel pulled by the small locomotives and it is hoped to extend the railway further in due course.

Leave the locomotive shed and walk down the steps to the washing floors to view the recently-erected wheel. Note particularly the series of ramps on the left divided by walls - these are the remains of the old ore bunkers and what can be seen are the hoppers down which the ore was tipped from the main adit railway described earlier.

Walk across the open area to the site of the wheel. A group of enthusiasts located the remains of what was the wheel originally used at Snaefell Mines. They negotiated its return to the Island and have erected it in a wheelpit which used to house a slightly smaller wheel which powered much of the machinery on the washing floors.

After browsing around the washing floors, cross the Laxey River just below the wheel and make your way out onto the Captain's Hill which climbs from Lower Laxey parallel to the washing floors. The objective is the tram station at Laxey. Get there by walking up Captain's Hill for a short distance and up a few steps through a gap in the wall on the left.

The setting for Laxey station is superb and this is as good a way as any to see it for the first time - from the garden of a pub! The Mines Tavern was originally the Mines Captain's house and it houses an interesting collection of photographs, in fact an ideal lunch stop. Even the bar looks like a tram.

Why not spend the afternoon in Laxey where you can inspect the Laxey Heritage Trust display adjoining the station before walking along Dumbell's Row to head further up the valley towards the Laxey Wheel. As you pass the Mines House dating from 1847 you can see clearly the cross cut adit to the mine.

After crossing Laxey River there is a small road to the right leading to a car park, turn into it but take the footpath off to the left and follow the signpost. The entrance to the Laxey Mines Trail, part of the Story of Mann, is at the top of the car park. There is a short underground experience which is still being developed to embrace more of the extremely interesting industrial archaeology of the area and it is well worth spending some time walking through the area. The modest entrance fee includes entry to the wheel.

There is a mill building opposite, now used as an engineering works. The browside tramway ran from the parking area opposite the mill up to what used to be a café adjacent to the wheel which was destroyed in a fire in 1985. No trace of the tramway exists today.

After your visit to the mines area return down to the road but before reaching it walk through the small gate on the left following the path past the cross cut adit to the mine and near to the entrance to the main adit, which is off to the left by the end of the mines railway. This is the point where the mines tramway entered the mine and ran for some considerable distance underground. Return to the tram station along the path beside the river. Cross over Dumbell's Row to view the statue of the miner on the opposite side and spend a moment thinking about the men who lost their lives in the Snaefell Mine. They died climbing down the ladders into foul air as a result of a smouldering fire in the mine.

If you have had enough walking for today then you can return to Douglas on the tram. If you are up for it you can take a ride to the top of Snaefell on the Snaefell Mountain Railway to view the Island from its highest peak before returning to Douglas. There are superb views from the comfort of the tram of Laxey Wheel and the Laxey valley with the Snaefell Mines and the whole of the north of the Island on the way. Oh did I say comfort; well you will have to enjoy wooden slatted seats as this is very much a Victorian tramcar despite being fitted with rheostatic braking!

A visit to Christ Church, Laxey at the station is worth making, if time permits. The history of this lovely little church set in what must be a unique setting is entwined with the mining history of Laxey. The village of Laxey, being within the parish of Lonan, was served by the parish church situated some three miles away. As with so many of the parish

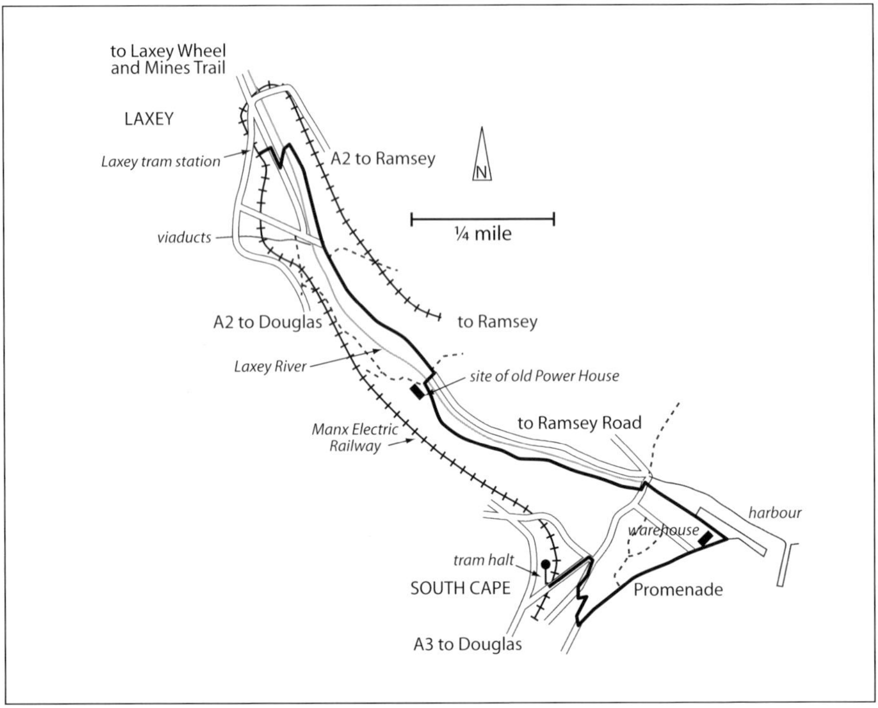

The Man Engine situated in Welch Shaft

churches, they were located in what was at the time of building considered to be the best position to serve the scattered rural community.

The village was a very busy place in the mid-1800s as a direct result of the mining industry. The population had increased significantly and with the temptation of public houses on the doorstep the need for a place of worship within the village was long overdue.

It is not surprising to find that the Laxey Mining Company and one of its principal shareholders, G W Dumbell, were instrumental in promoting a church for the village. Part of the garden of the Mines Captains House was made available for the church to be built right in the middle of the village. The church was designed by Ewan Christian and built largely by the miners themselves. The foundation stone was laid in 1852 by Lord Auckland, the Bishop of the

The Glen Road Electricity Generating Station

day. The church was consecrated on Tuesday, 27th May 1856 with due ceremony and the mines were closed for the day to allow the full participation of those for whom the church was built.

In 1917 Laxey was created as a Parochial District even though it was within the Parish of Lonan. It was not easily achieved and there were many meetings before the matter was satisfactorily resolved. The limited space on which the church stands meant that burials remained with the parish church. 1917 also saw the introduction of electric light into the church, another result of its location close to the Manx Electric Railway, who were the first generators of electricity on the Island.

Enjoy this small church built in the early English style with its interesting scissorbeam roof and simple internal decor.

The ruined remains of the buildings at Engine shaft

Laxey Wheel

WALK 5
RAMSEY

Travel to Ramsey by the Manx Electric Railway or take a No.3 bus. Walk from the tram station across Walpole Road and into Peel Street, turning down Market Hill to Market Place.

The tour of the town of Ramsey starts in Market Place opposite St Paul's Church, which dates from 1822 when it was spawned from the parish of Maughold as the town grew and the population centre gradually moved away from the centre of the parish.

The Market Place was the focal point of the town and the location of an open-air market selling predominantly fish in earlier times and even today on certain days market stalls selling various wares from fancy goods to vegetables can be seen.

Leave Market Place by way of Dale Street, passing the municipal swimming pool and on the left the Roman Catholic Church of Our Lady of the Sea, designed by Giles Gilbert Scott and built in 1900.

Turn right on to the promenade and walk in the direction of the Queens Pier. Dating from 1886, it is one of the classic Victorian Piers and was built to allow packet boats of the Isle of Man Steam Packet Company to call at all states of the tide. Now it is the subject of a campaign for its preservation. It did possess a tramway which ran the length of the pier conveying passengers and baggage to the boats.

Opposite the pier turn right up Queens Pier Road and then right again into Waterloo Road to return towards the centre of the town. Pass the Old Cross on the right. This was the site of the Old Town Hall and the point at which one arm of the Sulby River originally discharged to the sea. Just after the Old Cross note the distinctive Mysore Cottages, built to the memory of Sir Mark Cubbon who had been Commissioner General and Administrator of Mysore in India. Adjoining is the Old Grammar School dating from 1864 and only replaced by the present Grammar School in 1922.

It is interesting that Ramsey was the first place in the Island to experience Methodist preaching when John Merlin held meetings there in 1758. John Merlin had arrived by chance from Whitehaven and his real destination was Liverpool. John Crook was the preacher sent with the task of introducing Methodism to the Island and he came to Ramsey on 16th June 1775, the first of many visits made by him.

The first chapel was built near the Old Cross in 1794, not far from Mysore Cottages. A new chapel was built in Queen Street in 1812 and was acclaimed as the largest in the Island. By 1845 that too was proving to be inadequate and permission was sought from the Chapel Committee to build a larger chapel at Waterloo Road.

Continue to the present building situated on the corner of Waterloo Road and Parsonage Road which was built in 1846. James Callow, one of the original trustees, was involved in the building of this post-Wren auditory style church. This style was extensively adopted and retained by the Wesleyan movement long after it had been dropped by the established church. There are examples still to be seen in the Island at St. Paul's, Ramsey and at Athol Street Methodist Church, Peel.

Turn right into Peel Street and Bourne Place and Parliament Street, opposite the terminus of the Manx Electric Tramway. The building on the left as Parliament Street curves round to the left is the Courthouse and Police Station. Continue along Parliament Street and as you do it is worth looking up at the façades of the buildings to see the dates when most were built. The town still displays a good variety of shops in its main street despite the pressures of supermarkets.

Walk along as far as Christian Street before turning left, but pause at the junction and look ahead at the classic buildings of Auckland Terrace, now more than ever the business centre of the town. To the right, the old warehouses remain in different use but give a hint of the wealth and importance that this northern town once possessed.

Now turning left, you will see ahead on the skyline the Albert tower, built to commemorate a visit by Queen Victoria's consort when unable to land at Douglas. Walk as far as the junction with Albert Road and turn left again. On the right is Albert Road School which was built at the turn of the 20th century at the instigation of the newly-formed School Board.

At the junction with Tower Road turn right and at the end of the first terrace turn left down the narrow lane to emerge in the Manx Electric Railway Station. This was the rather ignominious end of the line when the tramway reached Ramsey after some protracted negotiation, instead of the grand entrance that the Tramway Company wanted along the sea front to connect with the Queens Pier. The tramway seems to have fared better than the pier and still provides a unique experience in travel for the visitor.

Walk through the station, taking care as trams move through the area, and turn right into Parsonage Road continuing as far as its junction with Queens Pier Road, turning right again and continuing past the bus station into Parliament Square. The newly-built Town Hall, replacing two earlier buildings on

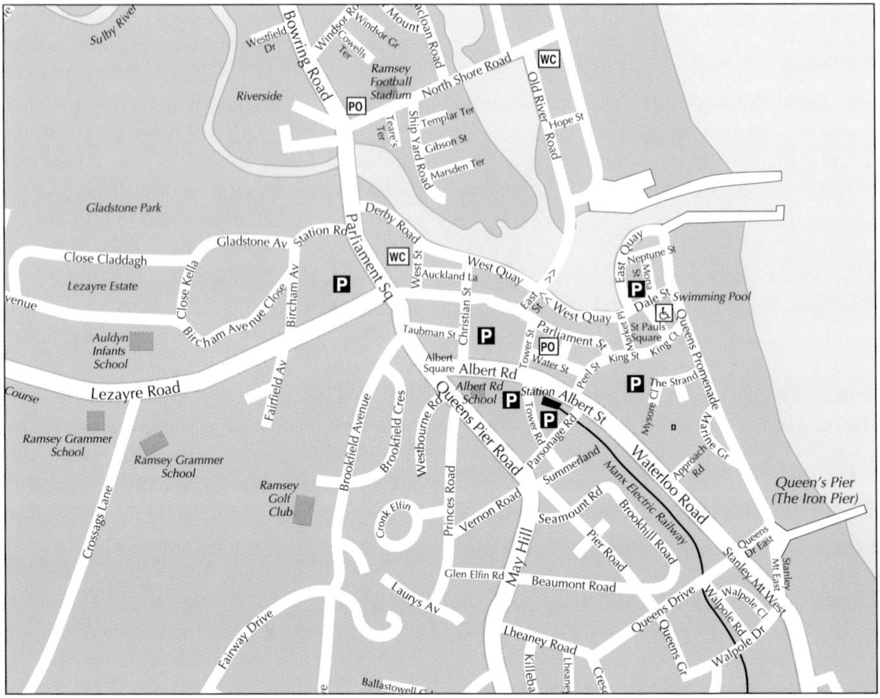

the site, was completed in 2003.

Continue along the road, which now changes to Bowring Road, and at the first roundabout pause to look across to the left at the area occupied by Ramsey Bakery. This was the site of the steam train station for Ramsey, but alas no trace now remains. Carrying on past the second roundabout cross the Bowring Road Bridge continuing straight on as far as Windsor Road.

Turn right and walk along Windsor Road. The style of the properties belies the opulence that the merchants and entrepreneurs who originally developed the town enjoyed when the town was in its infancy. At the end of the road turn right into Windsor Mount. Stop at the house on the corner and read the plaque on the wall proclaiming that the house was once the residence of T E Brown, the celebrated Manx poet.

Walk down Windsor Mount and Ballacloan Road to North Shore Road. To the left is the Mooragh Park, built on the site of the area where the second arm of the Sulby River originally discharged to the sea, whilst on the right you will pass the Ayre United football club ground.

Turn left on North Shore Road and walk to the Mooragh Promenade and then right to walk along the promenade which saw a late development in the Victorian guesthouse boom and never came to fruition like Douglas. All of the houses were built to a very similar design and have come to represent the symbol of the Victorian era on the Island.

Continue back towards the centre of the town crossing the swing bridge, so much a feature of the harbour. The harbour frontage ahead gives more of a clue to the past wealth of the town. Many of the old warehouse gables can be clearly seen, with just a few retaining their original use.

On reaching the other side of the bridge turn left on West Quay to return to Market Place.

WALK 6
GROUDLE GLEN, ONCHAN & PORT JACK

A 4km walk for which you should allow 1½ to 2 hours. The main objective of the walk is the Groudle Glen Railway.

Starting at the Derby Castle terminus of the Manx Electric Railway, take the tram to Groudle and be sure to sit on the seaward side to see the views of the coastline. Get off the tram at the Groudle halt and pause to look across at the Groudle Glen Hotel, which still retains much of its original character from the time when it was the terminus of the original Howstrake Estate Tramway.

Walk down through the Glen entrance and make for the terminus of the Groudle Glen Railway. This 2 ft. gauge railway was originally built in 1896 to transport our Victorian forebears from the glen out along the headland overlooking the sea to end above man - made pools which housed sea lions and polar bears.

Two steam locomotives were provided by W G Bagnall Limited of Stafford, both 2-4-0 tank engines and named SEA LION and POLAR BEAR, together with eight open carriages. Later, two electric battery powered locomotives entered service and also a petrol engined locomotive. After the Second World War, SEA LION was refurbished by cannibalising POLAR BEAR and the railway ran for some years before becoming derelict and abandoned in 1962.

A band of local enthusiasts set about resurrecting the railway and helped by apprentices from BNFL at Sellafield POLAR BEAR was refurbished and returned to the Island and operates on the now fully restored railway run by enthusiasts from The Isle of Man Steam Railway Supporters Association Limited. Over the years they have added considerably to the rolling stock and the locomotives. It is worth checking the timetable as SEA LION may be in steam, if so a ride on this novel line should not be missed.

From the Groudle Glen Railway station, return down the path to the river. The walk now follows the path under the stone arches of the road bridge which also carries the tramway to Laxey. Pause to consider how the local contractor, Mark Carine, constructed these substantial stone piers and the beautiful brick arches in 1894.

We follow the Groudle River which used to have a splendid stand of trees along the glen but many succumbed to severe gales in 2005. Follow the path which is boarded in several places to the Whitebridge crossing under the main Douglas to Laxey road on a walkway over the river and under the arch of the bridge.

The glen on the other side of the bridge is known locally as Molly Quirk's Glen. Continue to follow the river, ignoring the paths off to either side. The path joins another from the other side of the glen and there are some steps to the left which must be climbed part way before striking off to the right, continuing parallel to the river. A short distance further along the path cross a drainage culvert and a house at Little Mill comes into view.

Continue along the path and follow the steps down to a hole in the wall by the road. Turn left and after a few metres turn left again, following a steep public right of way to the road at the top. Cross the road and walk along School Road, passing Smiths Factory which manufactures precision parts for the aerospace industry.

Follow School Road into the village of Onchan. Turn right at the junction with the main road and cross the road opposite the Onchan Methodist Church. Take the next left down Church Road towards St. Peter's Church. The area is known as the Butt and forms the nucleus of the Onchan Heritage Centre. Take time to explore the village green and its wetland habitat.

Continue up the hill and enter the church gate. St. Peter's Church is the parish church and is an example of the community developing around the church, unlike many of the other parish churches where the parish church was geographically situated in the centre of the parish and communities grew away from the church.

The present church, built to replace an earlier stone-built church probably dating from 1408, was consecrated on 5th September 1833. When it was built the church had a flat ceiling similar to Lezayre and Ballaugh parish churches. Alterations in 1885 removed this flat ceiling and the exposed roof trusses were encased in dressed timber with additional decoration to designs by Geo. Kay, a noted local architect.

To celebrate the centenary of the church in 1933 an oak rood screen, made by Messrs Kelly Bros. of Kirk Michael, was added. The pulpit and altar rails were designed by the noted architect Baillie Scott, who worshipped at the church, and the modern stained glass windows were designed by Wilfred Quayle, who was at the time the Diocesan Surveyor.

The church is the place of worship used by the Lieut. Governors of the Isle of Man since the 1860s, their official residence being within the parish. As with all of the parish churches, there is a wealth of history written on the headstones within the churchyard. The church records date back to the early seventeenth century and the marriage records include those of Captain Bligh of the Bounty, who was married in Onchan Parish Church in 1781. In addition there is a collection of stone crosses in the porch.

Walk across the entrance to the church and take the path off to the right. Before following the path down through the churchyard take a look at the headstone to the right on the corner of the path, which is to G H Wood. The inscription tells you who he was. You may ride behind a locomotive named after him when travelling on the Isle of Man Railway.

Walk down through the churchyard and follow the pathway through the metal gate onto Royal Avenue, turning left to Port Jack at the bottom of the road, walking through the open glen to emerge above King Edward Road. The houses on both sides of the glen were requisitioned during the Second World War and became the Onchan Internment Camp, originally housing 1,200 German internees, although towards the end of hostilities the occupants were Italians.

Go right and then left down to the coast road and walk past a convenient fish and chip shop establishment. Why not stop if you are hungry?

Carefully cross the road here as there are trams to look out for as well as traffic and walk down the road on the pavement. Before returning to the starting point pass on the right the Manx Electric Railway depot which was built on the filled-in Port-e-Vada creek. The original power house can be seen at the back of the depot with the repair shops, whilst to the right are the modern running sheds. Finally, pass the site of the former Summerland complex, now demolished.

Back at Derby Castle I would recommend a look around the Horse Tramway Museum housed in the horse tram depot at Strathallan. Certainly open in the summer and if you are lucky you might at least see the exhibits, which include a cable car from the old cable tramway, through an open door out of season.

What better way to end this short walk than with a ride along the promenade on a horse tram and as internment camps have been mentioned briefly, see if you can see patches of asphalt in between the tram tracks where holes were made good when the concrete fence posts were removed from the promenade internment camps. Also look for the Falcon Cliff lift on the right as you approach the Hilton Hotel and Casino.

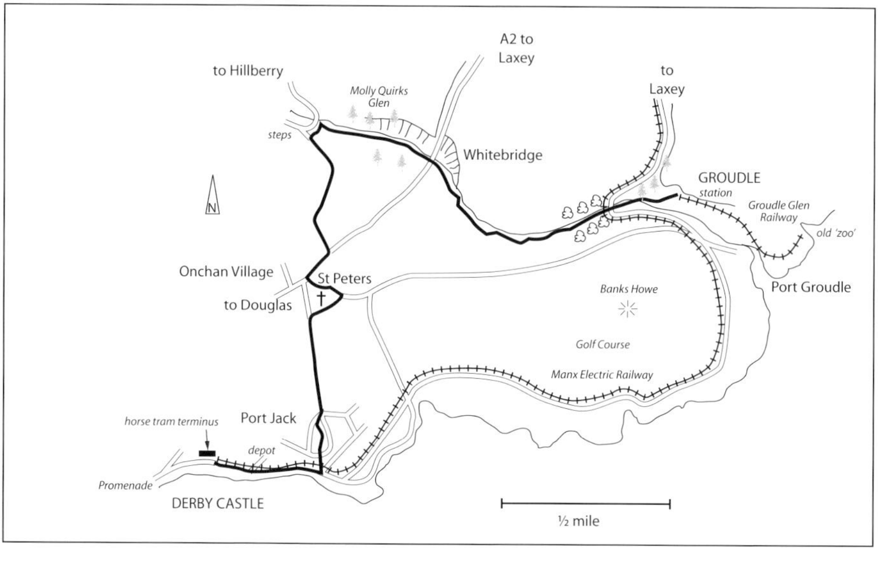

WALK 7
BAY FINE, THE SOUND & THE CHASMS

A 12km walk. Allow 4 hours. Refreshment is available at the Sound in the summer and at weekends in the winter. It is a scenic route with geological and archaeological interest. It is suitable for casual walkers or as an introduction to walking for anyone who has never enjoyed the pleasures of walking previously. There is plenty of time to visit the Railway Museum at Port Erin before starting the walk.

If you have never been to the Isle of Man before this walk should be the best introduction that you could have, even if you don't do any other walks. This is part of the Raad ny Foillan *(way of the gull)* or Coastal Footpath and described in more detail in the long distance walks. In the summer this walk can be idyllic and for the novice walker there is a choice that allows you to break the walk into two sections, returning to your start by bus.

To start your journey from Douglas, make your way to the steam railway station at the top of Douglas harbour. Take the train to Port Erin station, which is the terminus of the line. It is worth taking some time out if you take the first train of the day to look around the Railway Museum. Out of season you will have to travel south on a No.1 bus.

Leave the station and walk down Strand Road to the Lower Promenade and head off towards the pier and the lifeboat station. Cross the road here and take the coastal path up behind the former Liverpool University Marine Biological Station. In the early summer you can easily look over the wall above the buildings and if lucky you should see some young herring gulls on the nest. Through the stile at the end of the wall you can look across the bay towards Bradda Head and see the remains of the South Bradda Mines which produced lead and copper but were last worked in the 1880s. Looking south you can see Bay Fine and the Calf of Man in the distance. As you climb the path you will pass close to a fulmar colony. The climb is quite steep but the view from the top, both ahead and behind, over Port Erin and Bradda, is worth a pause for a breather.

The path follows the top of the cliff before dropping to skirt the hollow above Bay Fine. Keep to the slightly higher path which follows the top of an old sod hedge curving above the bay. The view back towards Port Erin is quite beautiful but even better in the winter in the height of a full westerly gale!

Over the top be careful not to miss the path, which is not well marked at this point. Walk diagonally across the open top of the headland, commanding a striking view of the Calf Island as you cross a boundary wall by means of a stile before descending the now clearly-defined path above Aldrick (*meaning the Old People's Creek*). Note particularly the fissured rocks - more of which later.

Ahead is an unusual rock known locally as "Jacob's Rock" which forms the foreground to the view of the Calf of Man. You can look down to the stony beach at Aldrick at this point before we climb up a steep section of the path between rocks and then down along the grassy cliff top to the Calf Sound.

Here is the new visitor centre and restaurant which was recently built by Manx National Heritage. There is a presentation describing the area in some detail and it is an ideal place to stop for refreshment. The restaurant overlooks the Sound, Kitterland and Calf of Man, which is now uninhabited and is a bird sanctuary. If you are lucky you may hear seals calling from the Cletts, which are a series of rocks to the left of the Calf as you look from the Visitor Centre.

In the summer, if you have had enough by now, you can get a bus back from here but take care as they only run every hour during the afternoon. Otherwise press on.

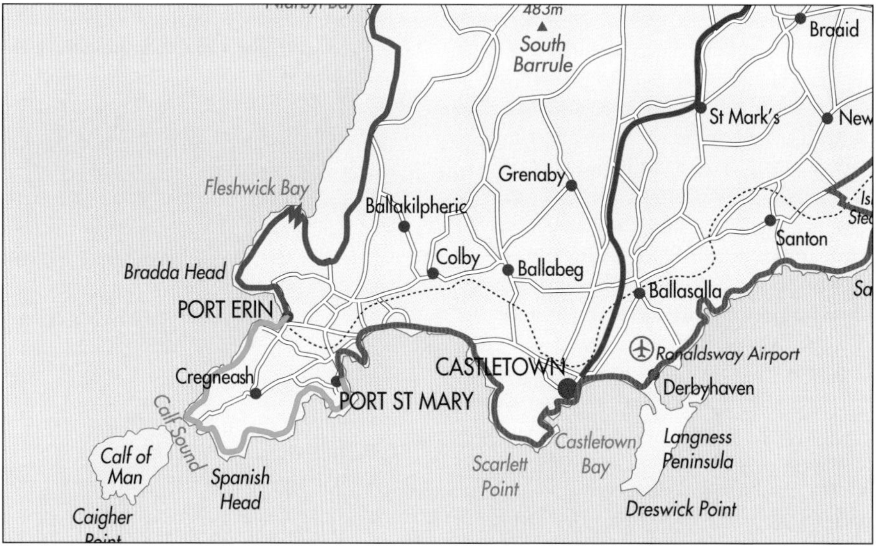

Suitably refreshed, follow the path along the parade, which is the open grass area, and make your way around Burroo Ned overlooking Baie ny Breechyn (*literally 'the Bay of the Breeches' so named by fishermen because the rock which splits the bay into two legs looks like a pair of breeches laid out*). Cross the stream, now made easy by a small bridge, to climb in earnest to the top of Cronk Mooar (*which just means 'big hill' although it has another name 'Cronk y Feeagh' which means 'hill of the ravens'*). I prefer this latter name as a pair of ravens range between here and Black Head. The view south from the top is magnificent with the Sound separating the Calf of Man from the Isle of Man and the small islet of Kitterland between the two.

Continue your walk over Spanish Head and Black Head. The path is close to the cliff edge at this point and although quite safe, children should be supervised. Looking south you can see the foreboding back face of Spanish Head with the tail of the Calf of Man behind it terminating in the Burroo, a quite distinctive rock which has a hole through it. You should also be able to see the Chicken Rock lighthouse which is no longer used following a fire in 1960. The lighthouse was built in 1875 to replace two earlier lights built in 1818 on the Calf of Man to a design of Robert Stevenson. Now they have all been replaced by a modern lighthouse built on the Calf in 1968. All the lighthouses are still there and a day trip to the Calf from Port Erin or Port St. Mary should not be missed.

Looking north, ahead you will overlook Baie ny Stackey, taking its name from the Stack or Sugar Loaf Rock which you will see shortly. The path is easily followed and as you close up on the cliffs ahead you will see that they are fissured, but more so than at Aldrick, and here they are more appropriately called the Chasms. Head for the disused building, once a café but now a shelter, and cross the boundary wall by a stile and opposite the shelter go through a small gate which gives access to the Chasms. There is also a small hill fort on the southern edge of the cliff.

Take care when viewing the fissures in the rocks. Take the path along the wall to the left as you look to sea, and follow it to an old metal kissing gate. As you pass through you will overlook the Sugar Loaf Rock and again the path is very close to the cliff edge. From here strike off diagonally to the left to join a defined track which can be clearly seen ahead. After a short distance crossing fields join a surfaced roadway which takes you towards Port St. Mary, which can now be seen ahead.

As you come into civilisation at Glen Chass take a right fork in the road, passing the dip at the Glen to take a footpath clearly marked through another metal kissing gate, crossing through the grounds of the former Perwick Bay Hotel, now converted to apartments. Shortly after leaving the entrance take a right turn through yet another metal kissing gate to follow the coast around Perwick Bay and Kallow Point.

Arriving at the harbour you can if you wish get the No.1 bus back to Douglas. The stop is next to the Albert Hotel!

However, if you walk another mile up Port St. Mary High Street past Chapel Bay, which I think is the nicest beach in the Island, and out of the village for about ½km you will be able to catch the train back from Port St. Mary Station.

WALK 8
DOUGLAS, MARINE DRIVE & PORT SODERICK

A 6km walk. Allow 2 hours. An easy coastal walk along the route of the former Douglas Head Marine Drive and Electric Tramway

Start at the Douglas Railway Station, go out of the main gate and cross the road to walk along Bridge Road over the Douglas Bridge. The first bridge was a two arched stone bridge. In 1930 the old stone bridge was replaced by a steel beam and concrete deck bridge. It still exists and can best be seen from the right-hand footpath on which you are walking. It has recently been extended on the opposite side as part of harbour improvements. Stop on the bridge and look upstream at the River Douglas, which is tidal at this point.

Cross the South Quay and turn left walking along the quay. The pier on the left between the river and the main harbour is known as the Tongue and is the oldest remaining harbour structure in Douglas, dating from 1700.

Continue to the next roundabout. Walk straight on, beside the industrial units of South Quay. Approaching the new lift bridge observe the tower on the right, which was the accumulator tower for the original bridge.

Carry on along the Approach Road to the Lifeboat House. It may be open, in which case it will be worth taking a look inside at the boat and some of the interesting history of the station. The present boat on station is a 47ft Tyne class lifeboat carrying the name of the

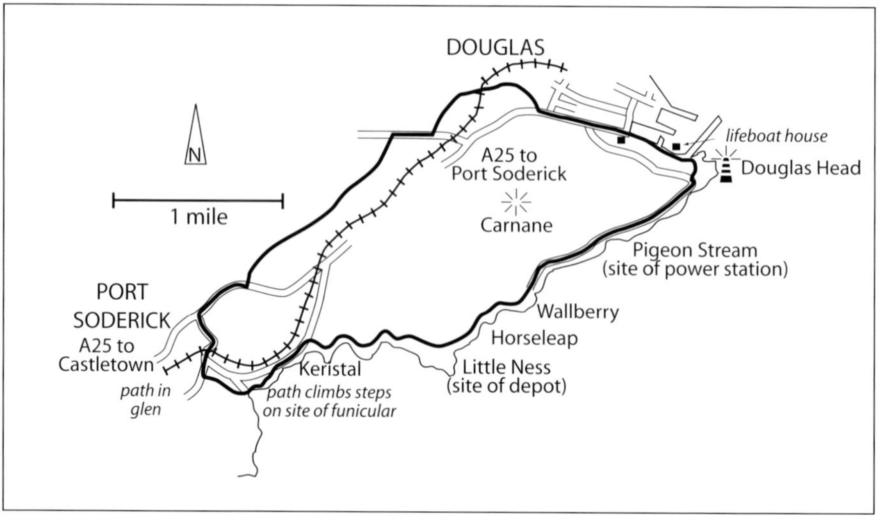

founder of the Royal National Lifeboat Institution, Sir William Hillary, who lived very close to here in 1813.

Walk along the road, past the fuel depot and walk to the right up the old road past the coastguard station. There is a flat area known as the quarterdeck where you can stop and observe the steps ahead and the slope to the left of the steps. This is the site of the track bed of the Douglas Head Incline Railway.

Go up the steps and as the path goes left here between two walls which carried the funicular track over the path you are at The Great Union Camera Obscura, recently restored to its former glory and open on certain days during the summer. If it is open go in and enjoy the Victorian delights of a camera obscura. Looking back over the harbour and the futuristic gas storage tank you can see the old breakwater built in 1879 and the new breakwater completed in 1982, which protects Douglas harbour from south-easterly and easterly winds.

Up the steps and you are at the start of the Marine Drive. Many of the old buildings on the head have been restored and converted to highly desirable apartments commanding a superb view over Douglas Bay. This was the site of the Douglas terminus of the Douglas Southern Electric Tramway Company Limited, which was constructed in 1896 on the line of an earlier marine drive roadway. The tramway was the only one built to the standard gauge of 4ft 8½ins. It was a single line with passing places and the line was on the landward side of the drive, which was very much narrower than today.

The Marine Drive came into Government ownership in 1946 and a scheme was promoted to build a modern roadway along the coast but it was to be 1963 before it was completed. Since then it has suffered from rock falls and toe erosion of some fill areas, which has resulted in its closure to vehicular traffic for the present. It is, however, open to pedestrians so off you go walking this section of the Coastal path in the opposite direction to that described in the long distance walks. The first feature you encounter is the remains of the toll gate and the ornamental arches are the only remaining tribute to the venture left on the Drive. The trams passed through the landward arch, horse drawn carriages through the other with pedestrians passing through a turnstile on payment of a toll.

After a short distance round a bend and cross an embankment near a small car park. This is Pigeon Stream and the car park was the site of the power generating equipment for the tramway. The boiler room, which housed two horizontal water tube boilers, was at the present car park level.

The two Browett - Lindley horizontal steam engines and generator sets were in the next floor down and below that a pump room with condensers, feed pumps and cooling water pumps. The site was chosen because of the ready supply of water from the stream. The first major civil engineering structure on the tramway crossed the inlet on the site of the present embankment and its total length was 35m. The original bridge is under the embankment and most of the fill material came from the power house.

In the distance the next headland has a distinct pointed rock known as the 'Nun's Chair' associated with penance punishment from the Nunnery built on the estate. Walk in that direction and rounding that headland you will come to the site of the second bridge on the route of the tramway. The original Marine Drive Company built a two span timber bridge to cross the ravine at Wallberry in 1893; this was replaced by a steel lattice two span bridge in 1896 with a total span of 78m. The present roadway by-passing the bridge was blasted out of the rock face and was completed in 1960. The masonry abutments and the centre pier can be seen from the new road alignment. It must have been an exhilarating experience travelling on the open top deck of the tramcar to spring off the edge of the cliff and cross the ravine at Wallberry.

The Drive is full of surprises and none more than the one you will get as you round the next corner and open up the view of the gully at Horseleap. On the short section of road between the two gullies there is a wide grass verge on the landward side and this is the last visible location of one of the eleven passing places that were on the tramway.

Once again the original Marine Drive roadway crossed the gully on a wooden trestle bridge, replaced in 1896 by a single span steel bridge of 36.5m on a gradient of 1 in 60. Again the original stone abutments can still be seen. The new roadway was constructed at these two locations using a cut and fill technique without constructing a protecting toe wall to stop erosion of the toe of the slope. In 1978 the fill on the seaward side of the roadway was undermined by the action of the sea and the resulting slips caused the road to be closed to traffic.

Round the corner and the headland on your left is Little Ness. This was the site chosen for the tram depot as it was the only area of land within the ownership of the company that was flat enough to accommodate the car shed just below the road and if you look in the shrubbery you may be able to see where the inspection pits were located. The gap in the fence is where the spur joined the four track depot to the main tramway line. The depot was originally served by a traverser, which was later converted to pointwork and was subsequently removed to Crich in Derbyshire, where car No.1 can still be seen in working order.

Looking ahead the view in the distance extends as far south as Langness. Round the next corner and here is another spectacular section of the drive. This is the Whing and it created considerable difficulties for the tramway company due to the difficult contorted rock strata of this section of the east coast of the Island. It is more visible here than anywhere else on the Drive and it continues to present problems with water penetration and frost heave causing minor rockfalls.

As you round the next corner the rock features of the Drive become softer and the original trackbed of the tramway can almost be seen. Leaving the Whing the tramway started to descend towards its southern terminus. Look over the wall on the seaward side of the drive and below is the remains of a Dutch coaster, mv Grietje, that went aground in a snow storm in 1963. Despite the attempts of the Douglas lifeboat the crew were eventually rescued by breeches buoy by the Douglas Coastguard.

The Drive continues a short distance to Keristal where the original roadway took the

Marine Drive

right fork to a further toll gate at the Old Castletown Road. Take the left fork across the head of the glen to continue south on the alignment of the original tramway. Look for the footpath sign on the seaward side of the road and follow it down to Port Soderick. The path starts at what was the southern terminus of the tramway, although short the path is a delightful piece of the coastal path.

Through a rusting gate you arrive at the top of a flight of steps which descend to Port Soderick which used to be a Victorian watering hole and even until recently retained some of its entertainment facilities. Walk along the promenade and follow the signs to the National Glen. Walk down to the glen, keeping to the left hand path, following the Crogga River right to the end. Join the rough road and turn right up to the highway and turn left. Follow the road under the railway bridge and uphill to join the Old Castletown Road and turn right.

As you arrive at Port Soderick village look for the right of way sign to direct you left along the ancient highway to Kewaigue, its entrance is obscured by new buildings but it leads off to the left at MR 347737. Follow it towards Middle farm. As you cross the stream look to the left and the sail-like top of the Island's incinerator and energy from waste plant can be seen. The building is an impressive modern architectural masterpiece. Passing the farm, join the main road opposite Kewaigue School. Turn right and walk down the hill alongside the Douglas golf course, turning left at the bottom of the hill before reaching the two railway bridges; the original bridge is to the right. Follow the Middle River towards Douglas and the Pulrose Power Station which is ahead of you.

The original power station on the Pulrose site was built in 1929 to supplement an earlier one on the quayside in Douglas (described in walk No.1). It has been extended and modernised several times since. The original station used steam-driven turbine generator sets, then followed by diesel generation. It has seen rapid development in the last decade, reverting to steam turbines for generation but now the steam is raised utilising natural gas and it is the principal generating station for the Island and yet another modern part of the Island's industrial history.

Near to the station you will come to a small bridge crossing the stream which you must cross to the right. The area was until recently a mixture of the old town tip and bog but it is now a burgeoning industrial estate. The road

The inaugural service of the Marine Drive Tramway

serving it severs what was an old funeral road from Douglas to the parish church of Kirk Braddan.

Cross the access road and walk between the security fences to rejoin the old road behind a warehouse. The road passes through the Nunnery Estate, an area which is full of history. It takes its name from the Nunnery of St. Bridget, the origins of which are uncertain and only the chapel of the old nunnery remains. The present house at the Nunnery was built in 1830 and occupied by the Taubman family and prior to that by Deemster Heywood. (A Deemster is the equivalent in the Manx Judiciary system to a High Court Judge). The Deemster's son, Peter, was born at the Nunnery in 1773 and he was a midshipman to Captain Bligh of the Bounty. Heywood was only 14 at the time of the mutiny but although condemned to death as a mutineer, he was subsequently pardoned as a result of his sister's intervention through Queen Charlotte. He later rose to the rank of Captain.

As you walk along the old road you will approach the point at which the Isle of Man Railway crosses at the start of its climb out of Douglas. Just before the bridge you can see an old stone wall curving from the right and this is the point at which the old road crossed the river. Pass under the railway bridge and note on the left the old sluice to the mill dam that fed the Nunnery corn mills. Walking a short distance beyond the railway you will come to a gap in the wall on the right which enables you to view an obelisk commemorating the Crimean War. You will emerge next to the ornate gatehouse adjacent to the Nunnery Mills dating from 1796 but now converted to offices. Records indicate that there was a mill on this site as early as 1643 providing flour and other products for the town of Douglas.

Now walk the short distance into Douglas alongside the river from which the town is named, derived from the combination of the two rivers which join at Pulrose near the Power Station. The river Dhoo drains the central valley and the river Glass drains the Baldwin valleys, and the two join to form the Douglas River. At the end of Leigh Terrace cross the Douglas Bridge and you are back at the Railway Station.

WALK 9
GLEN MONA, CASHTAL-YN-ARD & BALLAGLASS

A 4½ km walk, allow 1½ hours. It can be muddy in places. The walk takes in a mixture of pre-historic and industrial archaeology.

By tram or bus No.3, make your way to Glen Mona. On the way pay particular attention, after passing the dramatic cliff top journey round Bulgham Bay, to the Dhoon and the quarry on the right. This is Kion-e-Henin quarry, which was operated by the former Highway Board and described in the introduction. All of the buildings have now been removed but stone was moved by aerial ropeway to a storage hopper above a siding on the electric tramway specially built for the purpose in 1923. Some rail can still be seen and so too can the track bed on top of the hedge. Within the quarry there was a 2 ft gauge rail laid to take 'Jubilee' trucks from the face to the crusher. There are no remains of this quarry tramway but the ledge on which it ran can still be seen.

Dating from 1895 the Dhoon granite quarry lies on the other side of the main road. This quarry was leased by the same directors as the Manx Electric Railway venture and sets were manufactured for the Douglas Cable Tramway, later turning into a lucrative export venture. The quarry was connected to the Dhoon sidings by a narrow gauge tramway through a tunnel under the road and stone was provided for other tramway purposes.

On arrival at Glen Mona, get off the tram and follow the path down the glen to the ford on the Rhenab road, where you should turn left (this section of the path from Glen Mona has suffered from storm damage and may require a diversion) and walk along the surfaced road for approximately 1km. At a right-angled bend in the road, be careful to look for the signpost for Cashtal-yn-Ard by means of a short path from the road. Cashtal-yn-Ard displays the remains of a Neolithic five chambered tomb.

Returning to the road, continue downhill to Cornaa. As you start to see the houses of this little community be careful to look for a public right of way sign to Ballaglass and turn left uphill on a narrow track which skirts Ballaglass glen itself but affords a good view of some of the tallest trees to be found in the Island. Continue on the track until it enters a field alongside the tramway. Be careful to follow the waymarkers and cross the track with care. You will now see a very large building just below the track.

Ballaglass Glen

This is the remains of the Ballaglass power station (referred to in the description of the Manx Electric Railway in the introduction).

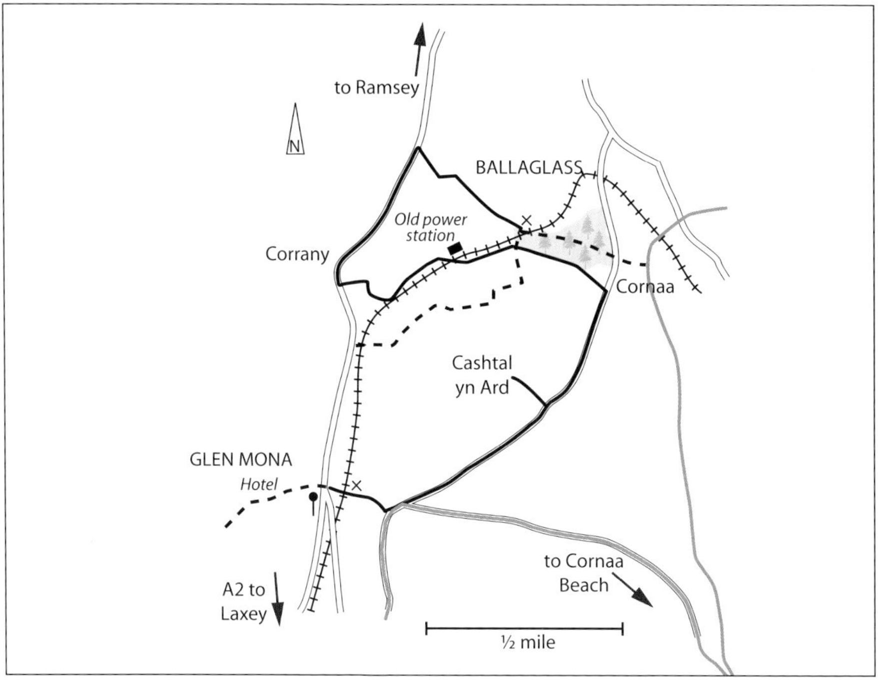

The two large halls housed the engines and generators in one and a stand-by battery storage system in the other. The buildings end-on to these were the boiler house and coal store. It is difficult now to imagine what it was like in 1898 since it has been converted to a private residence.

Imagine the activity in its hey day with two Robb-Armstrong tandem compound steam engines working on a pressure of 120 psi and generating 240 amps at 500 volts d.c. There were separate generators for battery charging, the batteries being capable of providing full voltage at 140 amps for six hours. Smoke from the boilers was carried up in a wrought iron segmental chimney. It would have made an ideal site for a transport museum but at the time of its disposal there was not the interest in industrial heritage that presently exists.

Moving on, follow the marked footpath to the Corony and care is needed as the path can be a little muddy in places. On joining the main road turn right down the hill on the main road and continue over the bridge at the bottom. Carry on up the hill and there is a pavement on the opposite side of the road. At the corner after Cardle Veg look for a right of way sign leading off to the right to return to Ballaglass halt, where the tram can be taken back to Douglas.

If you have time to spare take a walk through Ballaglass Glen admiring the natural gorge formed by the Cornaa River with its numerous waterfalls and the 17 acres of varied woodland. In the glen you will come across the wheelcase and office buildings of the Great Mona Mining Company. The workings were started in 1854 with levels at 10 and 24 fathoms, with some return of lead ore. The Great Mona Mining Company recommenced mining in 1866 and reached a depth of 50 fathoms (91m). By 1868 work was abandoned and the mine closed.

Winter saloon and open trailer passing Cornaa halt

WALK 10
ABBEYLANDS & NOBLE'S PARK TO LAXEY

For this 13km. walk, allow 4 hours. Eating facilities at Laxey with time to visit the Wheel and the Mines trail before returning to Douglas.

Using public transport from Douglas, take the No.5 bus to the Strang (MR 362783). From the cross-roads, take the East Baldwin road past the Strang Stores. The bus will have taken you through the recently-completed hospital built on the former site of the Lunatic Asylum originally built in 1867 and in use until recently as the Island's mental hospital.

After a short distance walking on the roadway a view of the central hills opens up with Greeba *(a Scandinavian word meaning a peak)* and Slieau Roy *(Red Mountain)* on the left with Slieau Karn Kerjol or more correctly Slieau Chiarn Gerjoil *(meaning the cairn of the devil)* on the right. The central hills will be described in more detail later, but this is a good place to stop, look at the map and identify the hills by name. Head for the saddle between Karn Kerjol and Mullagh Ouyr *(dun summit)* and the hut on the skyline is a good landmark.

Head downhill at the junction with the road to East Baldwin to Sir George's Bridge, named after Sir George Drinkwater, who had been a former mayor of Liverpool and contributed to the cost of building the original bridge. On the right is a flat area

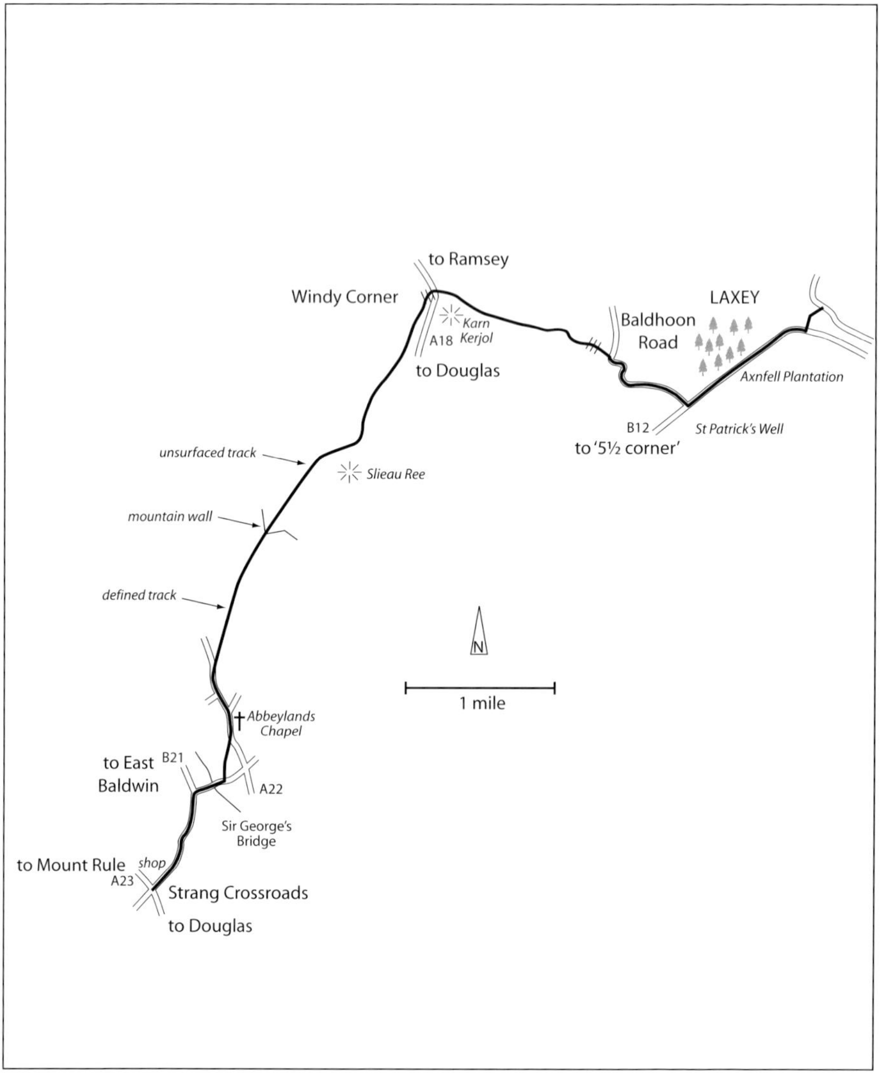

alongside the River Glass *(green stream)* which was the site of the locomotive shed, and a depot with four sidings, which was part of the West Baldwin Reservoir Tramway. You would have passed one of the quarries used in the construction of the dam on the right just before the bridge. The clay pit for the dam was at Ballacreetch which was on the top of the hill to your right on higher ground. To reach it the tramway used a reversing switch back or zig-zag and you will walk along part of it but there are no visible remains of the tramway.

A little further on cross a second bridge and turn sharp left following the footpath sign to Abbeylands and follow the track between the hedges. It can be wet and muddy at all times of the year. This is part of the route the tramway took on one of its zig-zags to gain height. Emerging at the top of this path turn left on the road and follow it for a short distance until you reach Abbeylands Chapel, where you should turn left again up a narrower surfaced roadway.

This roadway is one of a number of ancient highways in the Island, remnants of which are surfaced and in constant use, whilst the remainder are the domain of walkers and others engaged in outdoor pursuits. Don't be surprised to encounter motor-cyclists on these tracks - this is the Isle of Man and of course they have every right to be there. However, on this particular road you are more likely to encounter riders on horseback.

As you pass the farm buildings at Ballamenagh, be careful to follow the road slightly right and then straight on, ignoring the road to the left. The road quickly degenerates into an unsurfaced track with a predominantly white stone appearance and starts to climb up the southern slopes of Slieau Ree. The Manx gaelic name of this mountain is a little obscure as the Manx language was largely a spoken language and several meanings with the same sound give the hill the name of 'King's Mountain' or 'Red Mountain'.

As you come to the top of the defined track, the shape of the hill ahead is quite clear and I prefer to think of the hill as the Red Mountain - in autumn it is a rich purple and in winter a deep rusty red. Pause a while and look behind you and you can see Douglas and the harbour and an expanse of the south of the Island with South Barrule dominating the view to the right.

Cross the stile and enter the mountain land. The line of the old road is easily followed. It can be a little wet even in summer but the going, although on a gentle gradient,

is heavy under foot with heather and ling. Skirt the hill and you will see the Snaefell Mountain road above and ahead. The old road follows the curve of Slieau Ree and crosses a minor slip where care is needed to avoid losing the line of the track.

The old road then follows the Snaefell Mountain road and although it is never more than 100m away, the hustle and bustle of traffic passing the 33rd milestone on the famous T T course cannot be seen or heard at this point and as you walk through a small rock cutting you almost expect to meet a horse and cart coming towards you with its load of peat heading for Douglas.

As you come out of the cutting, you will have ahead of you a good view of Carraghyn *(a craggy place)*, Beinny Phott *(or more correctly Beinn yn oid meaning 'turf peak', it is pronounced as penny pot)* and Mullagh Ouyr. Head for the hut you could see earlier to cross the Mountain Road at Windy Corner. The hut is a marshal's shelter, used in June and September when the road is closed to traffic and used for motor-cycle racing. An emergency phone is located here and indeed at all of the shelters and in winter many motorists have been thankful for their presence. The Mountain Road in winter is exposed to gales and snow and can be a very inhospitable place.

After crossing the road, walk over the cattle grid and head off down the Noble's Park Road, which was built in 1860 under the terms of the Disafforesting Act following the sale of the Island by the Duke of Athol to the Crown. Enjoy the views of the Laxey Valley and the range of hills to the north from Claugh Ouyr to Slieau Lhean on the descent towards Glen Roy.

On joining the surfaced road, continue down into the valley. Stop and look over the hedge to the right and you should see some stone piers on the opposite side of the Glen Roy valley, together with some ruined buildings. These are the surface remains of the Glen Roy Mine, which was started in 1864 and lasted about 25 years. The shaft reached a depth of 122 fathoms (223m) and although some good lead and zinc blende was mined it was not successful. The stone columns supported a timber aqueduct which provided water for the larger of two wheels used for pumping and crushing.

Passing Riverside in the bottom of the valley you will have a steep climb up to the junction at Chibbyr Pheric *(St. Patrick's Well)*. Turning left, aim for the hill ahead, carrying straight on with Axnfell Plantation on your left. Soon the road starts to drop towards Laxey and as you leave the plantation be careful to take the footpath to the left, dropping steeply down into Laxey. Pause at the top to look up the Laxey valley and at the Laxey Wheel sitting at the head of the Glen Mooar valley where all the mining activity took place. If time permits while in Laxey, you should visit the Mines Trail, but if not there will be other opportunities with other walks centred on Laxey.

On the way down into the village, be careful to follow the path and you will emerge in the centre of Laxey opposite the Commissioners Offices, where a No.3 bus can be taken back to Douglas. A much more enjoyable alternative is to walk a short distance towards the tram station and return to Douglas by electric tram. As you cross the bottom end of the Glen Roy valley on the road viaduct, stop and look at the Laxey Flour Mills to the left and on the opposite side of the road another graceful arched curved viaduct which carries the tramway over the valley.

WALK 11
PORT ERIN & CREGNEASH

A 4km walk to visit the folk museum at Cregneash. Allow 2½ hours. Although this walk is a short one it is pretty strenuous.

Take the steam train from Douglas to Port Erin or a No.1 or 2 bus. Leaving the station, turn left into Station Road and pass the Steam Railway Museum, which you must visit later. Turn left and follow Strand Road to the Promenade. The view across Port Erin bay is superb, Bradda Head surmounted by Milners Tower to the right and the headland of Kione-ny Garee *(meaning the end of the thicket)* to the left and running across behind the Albert Pier is the remains of the breakwater which was destroyed in 1884 and which is referred to in the introduction in the section devoted to contractors' tramways.

Walk along the promenade past the recently renovated Bay Hotel and walk up the steep track alongside the building to emerge at the Darragh. Turn left along the unmade road until you reach the end of the row of houses and turn right up Ballnahowe Road.

You will soon come onto the open moorland of the Mull Hill *(or Meayll Hill meaning bald or bare hill)* and to the left of the road you can see a fenced area almost on top of the hill. Follow the path from the road to the Meayll Circle (MR 189677) a Megalithic monument containing a number of Neolithic burial chambers.

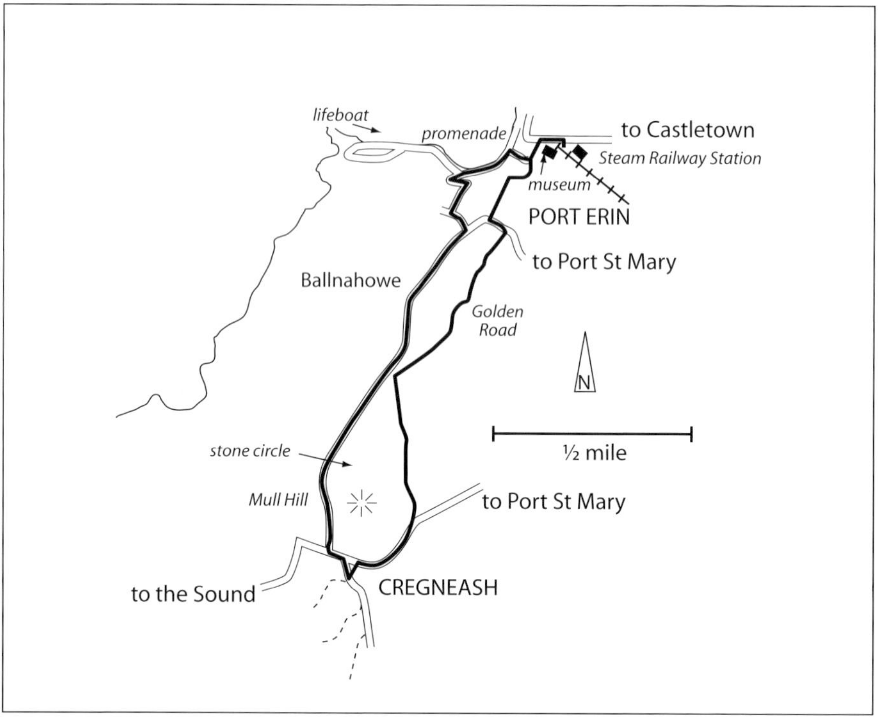

Walk to the top of the hill, passing the remains of the Second World War look-out posts. Follow the rough road to Cregneash village which you can see below, with its thatched cottages contrasting with the Civil Aviation Authority navigation beacon on the hilltop opposite. Ahead of you is a view over the Calf of Man and you can get some idea of its size from here. On a clear day you may be able to see the Mourne Mountains in the distance.

Cregneash *(derived from the Scandinavian Krakuness meaning 'crow ness', the old name of the promontory forming Spanish Head and Black Head)* is now preserved as a typical upland crofting village, also forming part of the Story of Mann and largely owned by the Manx National Trust and the Trustees of the Manx Museum, who maintain a number of the buildings as a folk museum. The farm is run on traditional lines and a short walk around the village with a visit to the visitor centre

Cregneash Church

IMR No.16 Mannin in the Railway Museum at Port Erin

and farm will give you an insight into a past way of life before you make your way back to Port Erin.

As you leave the village and join the Sound Road, turn right, passing Cregneash Quarry, originally a parish quarry, which is now a car park. The view ahead to the north will take your eye up the length of the Island. Port St Mary is in the foreground with the sweep of Bay ny Carrickey off to the right and Langness peninsula in the distance. The central hills forms the back drop to your view.

Be careful not to get carried away with the view as you have to take the right of way to the left by the mountain wall, just a short distance past the quarry skirting the Mull Hill. There are a number of ways down off the hill but I suggest you walk almost back to the Ballnahowe Road before turning down the 'Golden Road' to the right through Ballnahowe on a reasonable track which eventually peters out in a field at Ballnahowe. If you are careful you can pick up the waymarkers but if in doubt carry on down crossing over the hedge before reaching the houses. You appear to be in a private drive but don't worry, the right of way was there before the house! Turn right and down Baymount, left into St. Mary's Road and right at Ballafurt Road and you are back where you started. Buses and trains both leave the village from the railway station in Station Road.

Before leaving the village a visit to the Railway Museum which is open in the summer season is a must.

WALK 12
CASTLETOWN & ST. MICHAEL'S ISLE

A 6km walk for which you should allow 2 hours. The short walk to St. Michael's Isle is all flat and could be combined with the Castletown town trail.

Taking the train or No1 or No.8 bus travel to Castletown and the object is *to* visit the Castle. The bus will drop you outside the Castle or the railway station where this walk starts. From the railway station there is a short walk along the harbour to the town.

Castle Rushen dominates the town and its history is very much part of the history of the Isle of Man and the site was known to have been used by the Norse to defend the fertile southern lowlands. The Castle as seen now dates from the 14th century. It is more fully described in the town walk for Castletown. However, we are going to walk to St. Michael's Isle and visit the Castle later.

Leaving the station, turn left and walk to the roundabout at Janets Corner, going straight across along Shore Road to Castletown Promenade, turning left towards Derbyhaven, passing Hango Hill which is the site of the execution of William Christian for his part in the uprising against the Derby family in 1663. Take time out to cross the road and read the plaque giving a short description of the events of the period.

Continuing on towards Derbyhaven pass King William's College, a private co-educational school which will be seen more

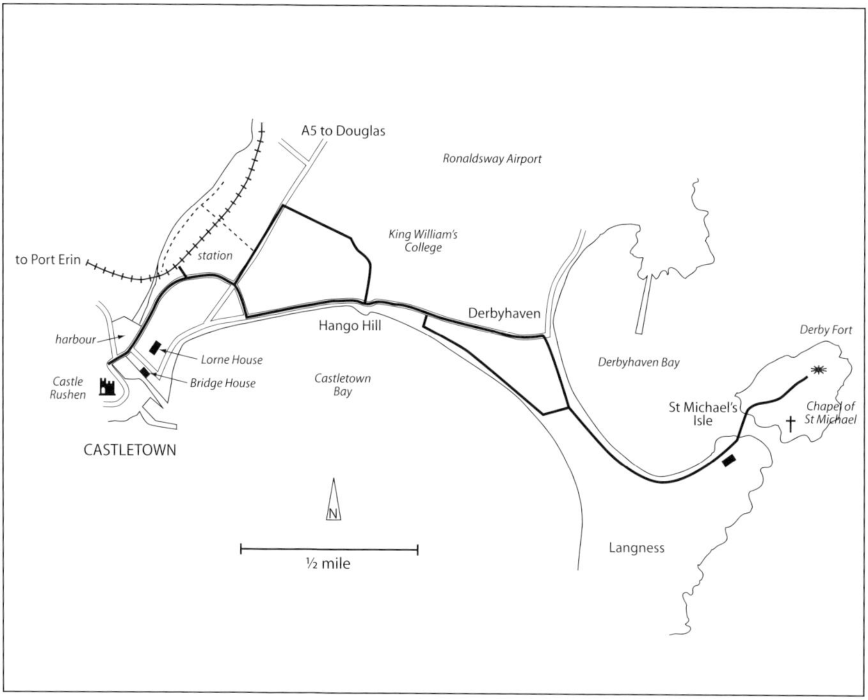

closely on your return. Also on your left you will pass Ronaldsway Airport.

At Derbyhaven turn right and walk out onto the peninsula of Langness, bearing left at the next junction by the ruined building. Continue round the sweep of Derbyhaven Bay towards the Golf Links Hotel. The area is always interesting with many small craft anchored in the protected water and oyster-catchers abound foraging on the edge of the tide. At low water you will often see a heron stealthily waiting his moment to strike. It is well to remember that you are walking alongside a golf course as play is close to the road at this point.

Walk past the Castletown Golf Links Hotel and over the causeway to St. Michael's Isle. To your right is the distinctive outline of the chapel of St. Michael dating from the 12th century and it is believed to be built on the site of an earlier Celtic Keeil. Continue round the islet on the path towards the round fort ahead.

This is the Derby Fort, believed to have been built originally as part of Henry VIII's coastal defences by Edward Stanley, the third Earl of Derby, at some time during the 16th century. The fort was repaired and strengthened during the Civil War to take a full culverain firing a 14lb ball and other armament to defend the Island from invasion by Cromwell. The work was carried out under the direction of James the Seventh, Earl of Derby, who was committed to the Royalist cause.

Admire the view over Derbyhaven and if the weather is favourable you will see a range of hills from Bradda to the left, the Carnanes, South Barrule, and Greeba. Make your way back the same way as you came as far as the ruined buildings.

Here turn left at the road junction. Walk straight on through the gate ahead, head straight for the sea and turn right along a defined track. Now change sides of the peninsula to walk around the edge of

Derbyhaven

Sandwick (Sanvik, another Scandinavian word meaning sandy creek). The area along which you are walking adjoining the golf course is the site of the Derby horse-races which were introduced by the 'Great Earl' and reintroduced by his son, Charles, the eighth Earl of Derby, after the restoration.

Join the road again near Hango Hill, crossing to walk back to Castletown through the grounds of King William's College, founded in 1668 by Bishop Barrow. The present buildings were designed by the architect, John Welch, and completed in 1833 and re-built after a disastrous fire in 1844. Take time to admire the architecture of the buildings but remember that it is a school.

Turning left at the main road, it is only a short walk back into the town to visit the Castle. At Janets Corner roundabout walk straight on and along the old promenade to the harbour and cross over the small footbridge to arrive at the Castle. Alternatively, the railway station is a short distance along Victoria Road to the right.

WALK 13
BALLASALLA & THE SILVERBURN

For this 5km walk, allow 2 hours. This walk, which is mostly in woodland, embraces a mixture of religious history and industrial archaeology. Take the train to Ballasalla or Bus No.1 or No.2.

The walk is centred on Ballasalla and the Silverburn Experience which incorporates a number of rights of way alongside the Silverburn River. A leaflet describing the various walks, which vary in length from 1½ km to 6 km, is available from Tourist Information Centres.

To do your own exploration of the Silverburn, start at Ballasalla railway station. Leave the station and turn right into Station Road and walk through the village towards Rushen Abbey. At the second roundabout look for Mill Road at the rear of Abbey Church and walk to the river. Crossing the Silverburn River, you can if you wish visit the grounds of the Abbey, now part of the Story of Mann, incorporating an historical garden, a visitor centre and a number of ruined remains of the original Abbey.

The Abbey was built by the Monks of Furness Abbey following a gift of land in 1134 by Olaf I, the youngest son Godred Crovan and King of Mann between 1113 and 1153. Although originally a Benedictine order, the monks of Rushen Abbey adopted the Cistercian principles, becoming active farmers and a dominant influence in the Isle.

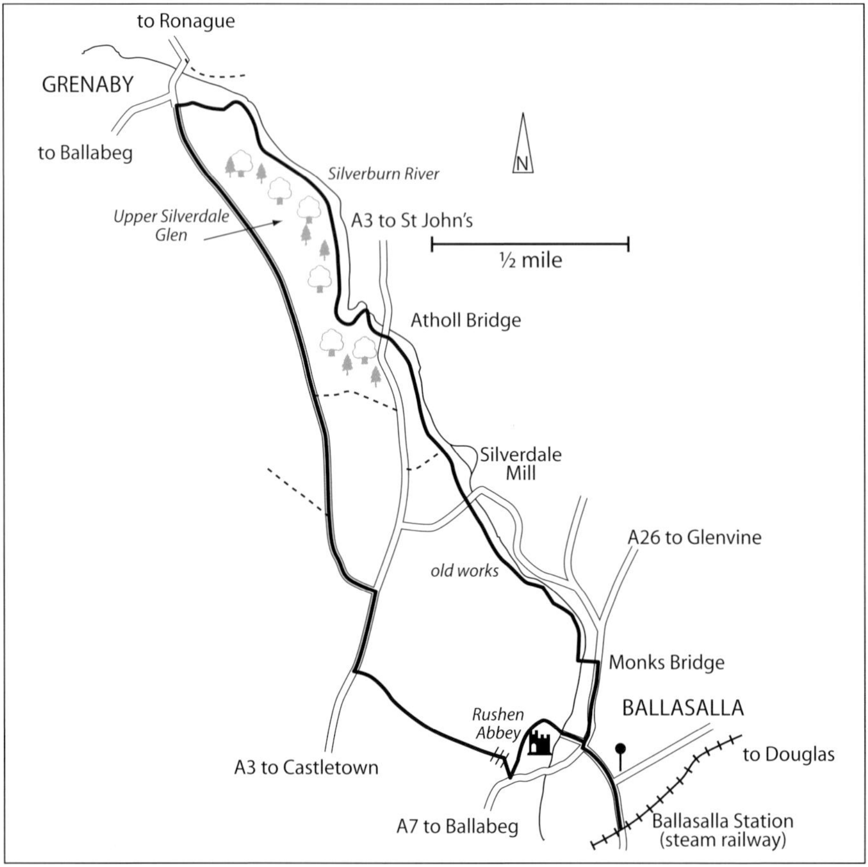

The Abbey was the last to be suppressed under the reformation, being dissolved in 1540. The Abbey tower, parts of the Sacristy and the Guest House remain.

Two Viking Kings of Mann were buried at the Abbey: Reginald II in 1250 and Magnus, the last Norse King, in 1265. By far the most important legacy from the monks of Rushen Abbey is the Chronicon Maniae *(the chronicles of Mann)* and the earliest written record of events in the Island.

From the Abbey continue straight on alongside the West Wall until you join the main road taking the public footpath to the right through the farmland at Ballahott with the lime quarries of Billown in the distance to your left where some of the oldest quarries and kilns in the Island can still be seen.

On joining the main road turn right and walk a short distance before turning left along the road to Grenaby for 2km, with South Barrule ahead in the distance. You can make out the rim of the rampart of the hill fort on its summit, which contained a considerable number of huts dating from 523 BC.

As you drop down into Grenaby be careful not to miss the path on your right which will take you back along a most beautiful part of the Silverburn River to Atholl Bridge where you will again cross the main road to continue along the Silverburn River, which is also part of the Millennium Way. As you approach Silverdale you will come across a boating lake and children's

Monks Bridge

playground with a café, which makes a pleasant place to stop and take refreshment.

The boating lake belies the earlier history of the old building adjoining the café. The building is the Creg Mill, which was one of two mills originally built by the monks of Rushen Abbey. The boating lake was originally the dam providing water for the wheel, which still turns. The roundabout is worth more than a passing glance as it too is uniquely water-powered by a wheel which was originally in use at the Foxdale Mines.

Suitably refreshed continue on downstream, following the waymarkers and passing the site of the Ballasalla Ochre and Umber Works, now converted to a private residence. The company was a sizeable one with warehousing in Castletown from which exports were made and the north quay still carries the name Umber Quay, a reminder of the past activity.

Continuing along the path you will shortly come across the Crossag Bridge or 'Monks Bridge'. Almost certainly the oldest surviving bridge on the Island, this packhorse bridge was built by the monks of Rushen Abbey and dates from the 14th Century. You are almost back at the Abbey and as you cross the modern footbridge to return to the village, you will pass the Abbey Mill, which was originally attached to the Abbey but now converted to residential use. It was a substantial mill with an internal wheel. Wander back through the village to return to Douglas by train or bus.

WALK 14
THE MICHAEL HILLS & WEST BALDWIN

A 21km walk. Allow 7 hours. It is advisable to take refreshments. This walk affords good views of the Island with some archaeological interest.

This is another walk in the northern half of the Island, embracing the hills overlooking the west coast. Leaving Douglas, take the No.5 or No. 6 bus to Sulby Glen cross-roads to start this walk.

After getting off the bus, cross the road passing the village shop and head up the Glen Road. Pass the village green of Old Sulby and passing a series of bends you will arrive at a small collection of houses. Look for the track leading off to the right between them. Head for Ballacuberagh Plantation, quickly gaining height and gradually emerging on the western slopes of Mount Karrin and the back of Ballaugh Mountain. As you join the open moorland you are still on an easily-followed track and soon join a surfaced road which you should follow for a short distance (approx. 500m). Here you will start to lose your view over the north with the very obvious landmark of Jurby Church right on the coast.

Be careful not to miss your way here as you leave the surfaced road at a shallow angle to the right (MR 633904) on a white coloured stony unsurfaced road, which quickly degenerates into a rutted track as it joins and follows the mountain boundary wall. You will pass Slieau Dhoo (*Black mountain*) on your right and can make a detour to the top to picnic. There is a stony depression which provides shelter and there is an interesting pond right on the summit. There is a good view ahead of Slieau Freoghane *(generally accepted as meaning Bilberry Mountain)* and Sartfell.

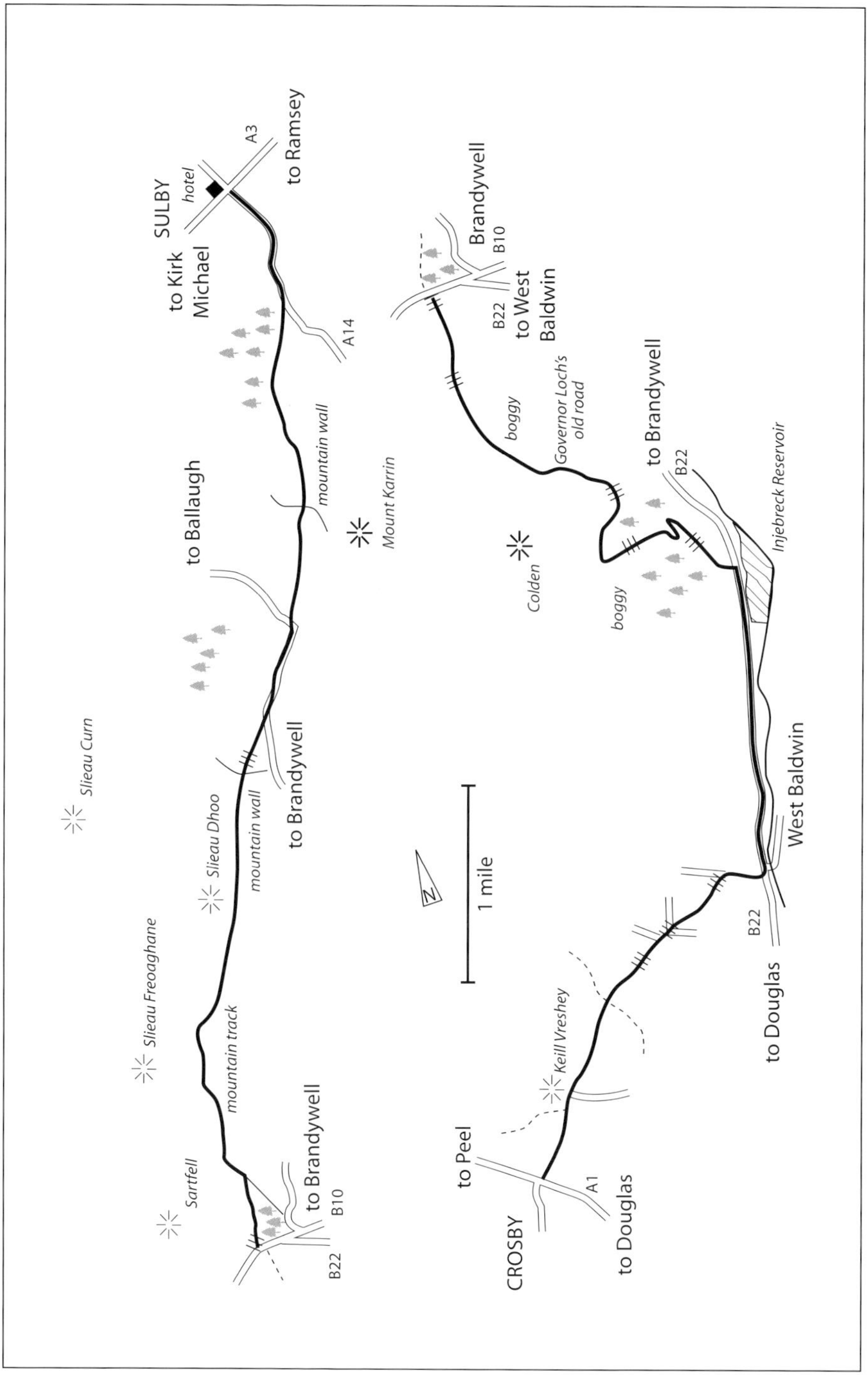
SULBY
hotel
A3
to Ramsey
to Kirk Michael
A14
mountain wall
Mount Karrin
to Ballaugh
to Brandywell
Slieau Curn
Slieau Dhoo
mountain wall
Slieau Freoaghane
mountain track
Sartfell
to Brandywell
B10
B22
N
1 mile
Brandywell
B10
B22
to West Baldwin
boggy
Governor Loch's old road
to Brandywell
B22
Injebreck Reservoir
Colden
boggy
West Baldwin
B22
to Douglas
Keill Vreshey
to Peel
A1
to Douglas
CROSBY

Looking towards Snaefell

Making your way back to the track, continue south-west, with views opening to your left of the Sulby Reservoir, which was only completed in 1983, with Snaefell behind it and the pointed peak of North Barrule to the far left. The valley immediately below is Druidale. Continue along the mountain wall until it turns left and follow it as the track becomes quite difficult to walk along. The view ahead now changes and you will see Slieau Maggle and Colden *(from the Scandanavian Kollrinn meaning the top summit)* ahead.

Join the Brandywell Road at a gate and turn left for a short distance before turning right on the track which passes the sheep pens on the side of Slieau Maggle *(which literally means the mountain of the test icles,so named because traditionally lambs were brought here to be cut and sheep pens are still used in the same location)*. The road is known as Governor Loch's road and although metalled and stone pitched it was never completed, which is a pity because as you will see it commands views of some magnificent scenery. It remains a public road but because it is now unsuitable for traffic you will find some unusual road signs apparently in the middle of nowhere.

Follow the road to a mountain wall and gate. Passing through the gate strike off left along the wide road with its hedges either side. It is usually very wet in the middle and impossible to walk on, except in winter when it is frozen. Pick your way along the bank on the right for about 1km, after which the road becomes more obvious and firmer under foot, cut on a ledge in the hill side. Skirting the shoulder of Colden you will have a superb view of Injebreck Hill and valley. You can make much better time now and the walking is easy as you swing round by the top of Colden Plantation and pass through some ornamental gate posts, which are remnants of the enclosures made by the Commissioners of Woods and Forests in 1860 under the Disafforresting Act.

Now enter the natural amphitheatre of the cirque on the east side of Colden, formed when the great ice sheet which covered the Irish Sea basin retreated and left numerous lakes in locations such as this. The cirque is more noticeable from a distance but is always a sheltered spot and a sun trap on a good summer's day and normally only occupied by a

few sheep. Cross over a stone bridge, now sadly partly destroyed by flood water, and head along the road for the plantation commanding a superb view of Carraghyn *(craggy place)* ahead. The road is very boggy again here and you must watch your step as you enter the plantation, trying to avoid going in over the top of your boots! If it is very wet, try up to the right under the trees. Fortunately it is only for a short distance, after which you can enjoy the walk down through Colden Plantation into the West Baldwin Valley.

Eventually you will come out on the West Baldwin road, opposite the Injebreck Reservoir built by the Douglas Corporation and completed in 1905 (refer to the section on contractors' tramways in the introduction). The undertaking was designed to meet the demands of the future and was without doubt extremely far-sighted, only recently requiring to be supplemented. Turn right and walk alongside the reservoir to West Baldwin village. As you approach the bridge at West Baldwin, you can see to the left traces of the formation of the reservoir tramway and another of the quarries used in the building of the dam. Just after the bridge join the Millennium Way and following the waymarkers walk through Ballagrawe and Ballalough, crossing a stone stile into a lane which you should follow for a short while before crossing a ladder stile into fields on the eastern flank of Greeba. With superb views to the left towards Douglas, head for the saddle between Greeba on the right and the small hill on the left Cronk ny Moghlane or Mucaillyn *(hill of the sows)*. The Millennium Way crosses over a track and down an unsurfaced stony road towards Crosby.

At Ballaharry, where the track joins the surfaced road, you can make a detour into the adjoining field to view the remains of the Celtic Keeill Vreshey, one of the many examples of Celtic Christianity which abound in the Island. The keeill was later known as the Chapel of St. Bridget. The Norse were eventually converted to Christianity and King Olaf II granted land in the vicinity of the keeill to the Priory of Whithorn in Galloway. Olaf II was the great grandson of Godred Croven.

Continue down the road to Crosby, which is the finish of this walk and where you catch a No.5, 6 or 6A bus back to Douglas.

WALK 15
SLIEAU RUY & RHENASS TO PEEL

A 18km walk. Allow 4½ hours. Full facilities are available at Peel and there is plenty of time to view the Castle.

Starting at Douglas, take a No.5 or No.6 bus to Crosby Church, getting off at the stop on the Glenvine side of the church. This is near to the point where our last walk finished but this time it will take you back uphill along the Glenvine Road, past Ballawilleykilley *(Killey's fold farm)* crossing the Mount Rule road at Corvonagh to continue to the top of Cronk ny Moghlane. The road takes a sharp turn to the right at the top of the hill and it is worth stopping to admire the view behind, across the central valley. You can see the lesser known hills that form the south side of the valley. From Douglas on the left with the Carnane prominent and easily distinguished by the TV transmitter mast built on the peak of the hill, the Mount and Slieau Chiarn *(Hill of the Lord)* almost ahead of you, and Creg-y-Whallian and Slieau Whallian *(Aleyn's mountain)* to your right.

As you round the corner another panorama of Island hills greets you and it is time to get the map out and identify them all and see where you travelled on some of the previous walks, with the East Baldwin valley below. Cross the path used on Walk No.14 and carry on uphill. The path gets steeper and rougher under foot as you climb under the bulk of Slieau Ruy. You will come to the

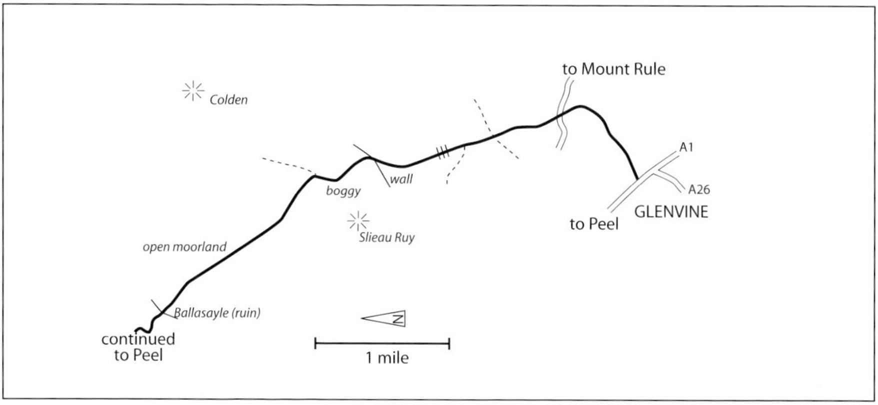

bottom mountain gate and as you walk on easier ground you will have a good view of Colden and the Creg over Eairy Vane and Eairy ne Sooie. Eairy means shieling and these upland pastures were where people would live with their animals during the summer months.

After passing the top mountain gate, you will find yourself on the open mountain but following a defined track. lkm from the gate negotiate a boggy area but shortly after this you will have to take care not to miss the signpost which shows where to go to get to Rhenass. A compass bearing of 310 degrees should get you over the shoulder between Slieau Ruy and Lhargee Ruy, otherwise go off at right angles to the path but resist the temptation to follow the very old track heading off to the left. There are markers which if you are lucky you should pick up. Anyway, once over the top you should see the shape of a large stone sheep pen characteristic of the old crown and common lands and that is where you are heading.You will see that the pen is in the shape of letter D and you want to walk along the straight wall of it to pick up the line of an old track which will lead you over the open moorland to Rhenass. There are concrete markers on the line of the path but again if there is any doubt head for the dip in the line of the hills ahead and eventually a white house will come into view, which is a perfect landmark.

As you walk across this area which is on the western flank of Lhargee Ruy *(the red slope)* you can see to the left the prominent shape of Corrin's Folly on Corrin's Hill above Peel and closer to hand the head of Glen Helen, one of the Island's prettiest national glens. As you approach the end of the moorland, cross to the right-hand side of the track which quickly develops into a gully, and

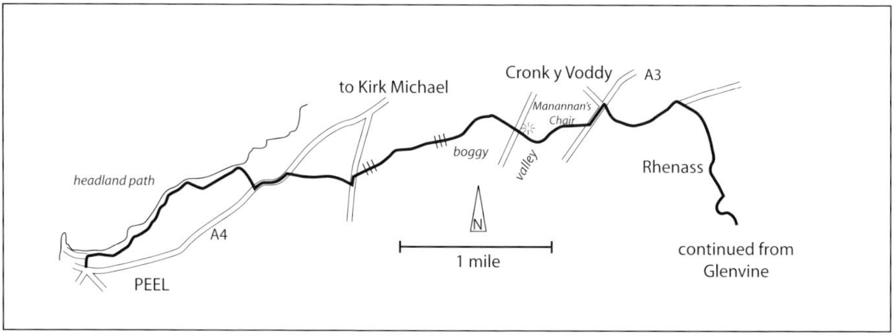

View north over Cass Struan

aim for the gate in the corner, which is really the line of the road which is now more apparent between hedges. After a short distance turn right through a gate past the ruins of Ballasayle *(Sayle's farm)*. As you pass you can see one of the best surviving examples of a horse mill.

Follow the track down to the stream which you can cross on the stepping stones. Cross over the little stone bridge at Mullen Rhenass and follow the road to the junction with the Little London Road and turn left to follow the surfaced road to Cronk y Voddy *(meaning hill of the dog)* crossroads. Go left here on the main road and this is one of those areas I mentioned at the start that is a no-go area on certain days in June and September.

After a short distance pick up the sign to Manannan's Chair on the other side of the road and walk across an unusual upland valley hardly noticed normally as you head for the Staarvey Road *(Staarvey meaning a rough shallow ford)*. Cross the road through the gate and follow this very wet muddy track past Lherghycholvine, passing the remains of a number of tholtans giving silent homage to a past way of life. The view over Peel and the ultimate destination is rewarding as you descend to the Knocksharry Road and cross over it, taking the road through the farm at Lhergydhoo *(the black slope)*. Pass over the old railway line that used to run to Ramsey before meeting the coast road.

Turning left, walk a short distance along this road before going through a white stile on the right to take the headland path to Peel, part of the coastal path, arriving on the promenade and having enjoyed views of the Castle on St. Patrick's Isle. It is worth walking round to the Castle if time permits. Although now largely in a ruinous state, it is interesting to view the ancient cathedral which pre-dates most of the rest of the remains dating from circa 1390. Excavations between 1982 and 1990 have revealed Norse and pre-Norse Celtic settlements on the Islet.

Returning from the Castle to the town centre, you will pass some of the older kipper houses for which the town is famous and in season the whole of the harbour is covered in a haze of smoke from the oak chippings still used in the curing process. A call at the Creek Inn for refreshment is a welcome break before making your way up Station Road to Michael Street and Derby Road for the bus back to Douglas.

WALK 16
CROSBY, CORNELLY MINES, FOXDALE & ST JOHN'S

This is a 12km walk. Allow 3 hrs. The walk touches on a number of industrial archaeological remains of the Foxdale mining activity and finishes at historic St. John's. This walk can be wet and muddy in winter.

This time take the No.6 or No.5 bus from Douglas as far as Crosby, getting off at the Post Office at Crosby.

Turn left down Old School Road, which used to be called Station Road, and as you pass the playing fields on your right, you will come to the site of the former Crosby railway station. Turn right and follow the signs indicating the Railway Heritage Trail, which is overlapped for a short distance (see walk No19). Pause and imagine the activity at this station, with its cattle dock and goods shed. Even in the last years of operation trains were scheduled to pass at this station.

Head off in a westerly direction along the former track, passing on the left the main engineering works depot of the Department of Transport. This was built on the site of an old quarry which provided stone for highway construction and which can be seen behind the buildings.

The former railway track ran through the central valley from Douglas to Peel and the section on which you are walking was built on extremely boggy land or Curragh. As you walk under the stony outcrop of Creg y

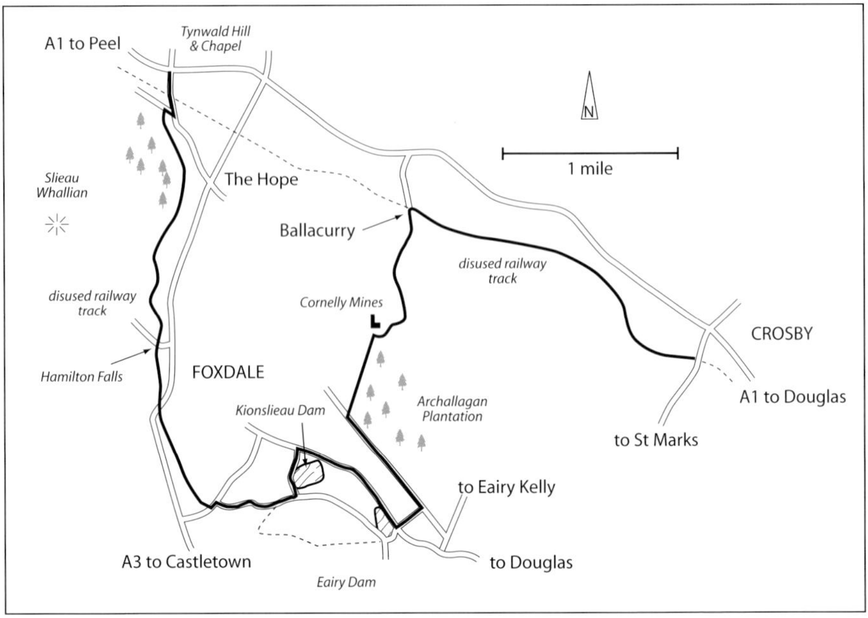

Whallian, having passed Cooilingel crossing, you can really see the natural vegetation of the curragh on your right.

The hill to your right is Greeba *(derived from the Norse meaning the peak)* 423m, with Slieau Ruy further to the right. The next road crossing is at the Ballacurry *(marsh farm)* road and here is where you leave the railway track and turn left, walking through the farmyard and up the surfaced road between two hedges.

After a short distance, come out from between these hedges and you will be on a slight plateau overlooking Greeba Mountain. Looking east down the central valley, it certainly presents one of the best views of Greeba. Look carefully amongst the trees on Greeba to find a castle in the trees. It was the one-time residence of Hall Caine, the celebrated Manx author.

Having had a breather, start to climb in earnest, being careful to take the sharp right turn and continue up between the overgrown hedges either side of what has now become a very rough stony track. At the top of the hill the view opens out and to your right ahead is the Townsend or Cornelly Mines where you can stop and look at the surface remains.

The mine was worked prior to 1845 but the present buildings date from 1878 and operations stopped in 1886. There were two shafts dug 12 fathoms (22m) apart. Engine shaft was the deepest at 140 fathoms (254m) A high quality galena was found, together with some semi-precious crystal.

There was an earlier shaft, known as the Mountain shaft, some distance east of the present remains which was abandoned when the new engine shafts were sunk. The largest building is the remains of the engine house at the head of the New Engine Shaft which connected at 80 fathoms (146m) to the Old Engine Shaft.

Leaving the mines, walk uphill on the surfaced road, passing Cornelly House and Archallagan Plantation on your left. Look right to see the outline of Slieau Whallian tops and your walk will take you back to St. John's under its flank. At the junction at the top of the hill, turn left skirting the plantation and after about 1km, just before reaching Manx Radio's medium wave transmission masts, turn right through the trees down a waymarked path, crossing a road serving some houses. At the bottom of the path you will reach the Eairy *(sheiling)*. Turn right, taking care to walk straight ahead at the next corner following the Lhoobs Road with the Eairy Dam on your left. It is always worth stopping at any time of the year to see what bird life is on the water; ducks and geese are always there. You may see the occasional heron, swans and the inevitable gulls. Migrant birds can be seen too and in the winter when the dam is frozen swans and geese become confused and land in a sliding flurry of wings and feathers before coming to a bemused stop.

The dam was built to provide water for the Far Gin Mine (later to become the Central Foxdale mine) and the associated saw mill. Workings started in the early 1820s but came to a halt by 1860. The workings were re-opened in 1871 and work was concentrated on three shafts, Elizabeth, Amy and Taylor's, which reached depths of 145, 40 and 74 fathoms. The mine was productive and the lead ore had a high silver content.

Continuing along the road you will see a second dam which was also built to provide water for the numerous water wheels at the Foxdale Mines and this walk will take you across the head of the dam. Turn left off the road over a stile and walk along the edge of the plantation to emerge briefly in the open, overlooking the water of the Kion Slieau dam. Join the main road and turn right to walk towards Foxdale Village.

On your left are the surface remains of the spoil heaps and washing floors associated with Potts shaft. Note the clock tower on the corner as you come into the village. When mining came to Foxdale it brought with it a tremendous increase in population. Public houses sprang up in its wake and it soon supported a constable and a jail. Methodism found a strong footing in the area, as in Laxey.

The established church appointed a chaplain to Foxdale in 1850 but it was to be 1881 before Foxdale had its own church. Public subscription and a handsome donation from the mining company resulted in the foundation stone being laid in 1874 by Mrs. Cecil Hall. The church, designed by James Cowle, was consecrated by Bishop Rowley Hill on Whitsun Tuesday, 7th June 1881 as a chapel of ease to Kirk Patrick Parish Church. The village became a parish district in its own right some years later. The church can be seen on the opposite side of the valley beyond the old school as you walk down the disused railway track.

It is hard to imagine now what this area was like at the height of the mining boom, with lead and silver being produced to an annual value of £50,000 at the time that the railway was built. There were 350 people employed in the mines. The three main shafts in Foxdale were Potts, Beckwiths and Bawdens. The deepest was Beckwiths, which reached a depth of 320 fathoms (1920 feet) by 1902 and yet by 1911 the industry had declined and the Isle of Man Mining Company had ceased working.

The next objective is the railway station next to the school. The Foxdale Line was built in 1886 by the Foxdale Railway Company, an offshoot of the Manx Northern Railway as an opportunist venture to win lucrative mineral traffic from the Isle of Man Railway. Prior to the building of the railway to Foxdale, all the ore was taken by horse and cart to St. John's for onward transmission by the Isle of Man Railway to Douglas Station. It then had to be loaded again into horse-drawn carts and taken to the harbour at Douglas. The contract for the carriage of the ore came up for renewal and the Manx Northern bid was successful.

With the Foxdale Railway completed and with access into the mines, together with a direct line to Ramsey harbour over the Manx Northern Railway metals, the contract was won. It was to become a financial burden to the Manx Northern, leading to its eventual downfall. In the end everything came into the ownership of the Isle of Man Railway.

Starting by the old station building,

IMR No 8 Fenella at Foxdale terminus with the mines' spoil heaps to the right

which is opposite the school in Mines Road, the walk is all downhill at a steady gradient of 1 in 49. There is quite a wide defined track which runs from the road beside the school. This is the start of the track bed and the building on the left is the station building. There was a shallow platform with brick edging served by a single line with a run round loop. The area presently occupied by the school was the site of the principal spoil heap from Beckwiths mine. A temporary siding was built into this area in the 1930s to assist with the removal of this spoil, which was mostly used in the construction of the playing fields which now form the basis of the National Sports Centre in Douglas (see the Heritage Trail walk). The spoil from Bawdens shaft formed a massive spoil heap behind the station which was hemmed in between these two mountains of waste - very different from today and very difficult to imagine.

Beyond the station building there was a small brick structure supporting a water tank for the locomotives. A single line climbed behind the back of the station at a gradient of 1 in 12 to cross the road and enter the mines yard, where the ore was loaded into the wagons for Ramsey via St. John's. This line was always referred to as 'the back of the moon', an apt description if you had seen the area after the mines had ceased working. Before you start your walk you should just walk up Mines Road a short distance where the line crossed the road and you should be able to see the remnants of the crossing with the running rails and check rails in the road surface, the only visible remains of the Foxdale Railway.

Returning to the Station, you now start your walk down the line. While the first part near the school is somewhat changed, you will soon come onto the old track-bed, which is quite unmistakably railway as it skirts behind the miners cottages in Higher Foxdale. On the hillside to the right there are still some visible remains of the oldest mine in the area, particularly near the river.

Now you are very close to the road. The line ran on a high stone-built embankment before swinging left to cross the road on a steel girder skew bridge (*Lukes Bridge*), the road meanwhile prescribing a double corner as it dropped under the bridge to continue to Lower Foxdale (*The name Foxdale is an anglicised corruption of Forsdalr a Scandinavian word meaning waterfall dale*). The bridge was removed when the track was lifted in the early 1970s. Climb through the stile in the boundary wall and cross the road to the opposite side where there are steps leading up the old bridge abutment and back to the track-bed.

Now the formation can be really appreciated. Continue on an embankment towards Lower Foxdale with a view of Slieau Whallian ahead. Cross over the accommodation road to Ballamore farm (*from an Irish family name - More's farm*) on a small bridge. The line entered a cutting through rock as the line curved left and approached Waterfall Halt, which was the only intermediate stop on the line. At Waterfall little remains to show what was there. Originally planned to have a passing loop, it was completed with only the single running line and a small wooden building on the flat area to the right.

Carry straight on, crossing the Gleneedle stream which is a tributary of the Foxdale River. You will be able to see the abutments of an old railway bridge as you cross the stream. The halt served the community of Lower Foxdale and also attracted visitors to the Hamilton Falls where the stream cascades down a rock face before joining the main river.

Walk under the road overbridge carrying the Ballanass road over the railway (*Balla n eas Manx Gaelic meaning farm of the waterfall*). You are in a short cutting under trees and can probably hear the sound of the waterfall below you on the right. Emerge to curve around the hillside with lovely views towards the central valley dominated by Greeba Mountain. The line was built on an embankment and followed the natural lie of the land. There was an old mine on the left but nothing remains but a very overgrown spoil heap. The occasional telegraph pole is a reminder of the railway.

You are now approaching Slieau Whallian farm (*an obscure word which could refer to a personal name, possibly Mc Aleyn, or it could refer to hill of the whelps*) and entering a wooded area. Pass under the bridge carrying an accommodation road associated with the farm and you will see that the construction was of a very simple nature and used concrete for the abutments. After the bridge the line passes through a very attractive section before curving left alongside the plantation which is part of the larger Slieau Whallian plantation - not there of course when the railway was built.

Unfortunately you have to leave the line at the end of the plantation and veer off to the left and join the Slieau Whallian back road which you should follow to the right downhill to the Patrick Road and right again to the next junction.

Before leaving the track-bed it is worth looking where the track continued on an embankment which was almost forty feet high. Although now much overgrown, it still gives an indication of the amount of material needed for its construction. The line curved to the right to cross the Foxdale River on two steel spans carried on a central stone pier between two abutments.

If you turn right at the junction and walk a short distance towards the Hope you will see where the line crossed the river after which it curved around in a left-handed sweep to cross over the Peel Line and into St John's. Returning to the junction with the Patrick Road, carry on towards the village as far as the Farmers Arms and look to the right over the open area which was the site of the St. John's Station, originally built by the Isle of Man Railway. The rather Spartan station building was situated where the new sheltered housing encroaches on the area. It is very hard to imagine what it was like just forty years ago. This is the area referred to earlier as the Island's Crewe Junction.

Two lines crossed the road on a level

St John's Railway Station in 1965

crossing, one bound for Peel and the other nearest to Tynwald Hill bound for Ramsey. There were two platforms with four tracks, a number of sidings and a signal box and behind that a large carriage shed. Now the new primary school occupies most of this area and the site of a sand pit which was used for sand and gravel extraction by the railway.

Walking further up Station Road, cross over the Foxdale line just before the Post Office. Look over the right-hand parapet wall and see where the line came into St John's behind Pretoria Terrace with the embankment climbing away towards Foxdale and over the Peel line. Looking over the left-hand parapet, you can clearly see the St John's terminus of the Foxdale railway. The station was a grand building by comparison with that belonging to the Isle of Man Railway and is used as a private dwelling. It was similar in style to the station building at Foxdale. There was a passing loop at the station with goods sidings and the connection to the Manx Northern Railway beyond.

Join the main Douglas to Peel road opposite Tynwald Hill and it is from here that you can catch the bus back to Douglas. First have a look at the Hill, which is a four-tiered assembly place based on the Norse 'Thingvollr' (The Parliament Field) where the annual midsummer parliament has been held on 5th July since the period of the Norse Kingdom of Man and is still held to this day.

Walk along the processional way to St. John's Church and in the field behind the Church you will find the Millennium Stone which was erected to celebrate the one thousand years of government in the Island in 1979. To find out more about the Island's unique form of Government you must visit the National Museum in Douglas.

WALK 17
GLEN MAYE, GLEN RUSHEN & ST JOHN'S

Take the No.5 or No.6 bus to Peel and then the No.7 bus to Dalby, getting off at Glen Maye. Allow 3½ hrs for this 13km walk which embraces more of the industrial heritage of the island.

Starting at Glen Maye village, walk down the hill past the Waterfall Hotel as far as the dip at the bottom and take the left-hand fork along the Sound Road, being sure to go straight on ignoring the signs for the Bayr Skeddan and taking care when arriving at the farm to follow the sign 'road unsuitable for motors' and take the rough stony path to the right between the hedges.

All the walks have their ups and downs but this one seems to have more than its fair share! Soon the road starts to climb steeply up between the hedges and can often be wet and muddy under foot. Eventually the path emerges onto Dalby Mountain, follow it to the top gate. Be careful here as there are three tracks. Follow the one on the right against the hedge.

The track can be very muddy in winter so it is best to walk on top of the hedge. About ½ km along the track be careful again to cross over the fence on the stile and follow the track more or less straight ahead. If in doubt aim straight for the top of Cronk ny Arrey Laa, which is a good land mark. The track can be difficult to follow when the gorse is in full bloom but the track can be made out stretching ahead across the open moorland to join the surfaced road leading

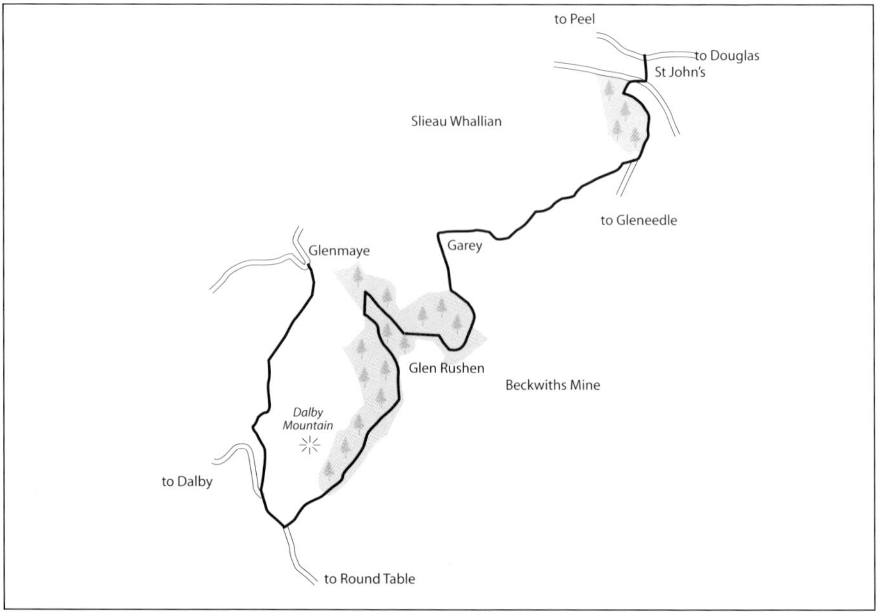

from Dalby to the Round Table Crossroads, which comes into view below on the right. There are occasional waymarkers on concrete posts on the route of the path.

Turn left at the road and walk along it for another ½ km looking for a gate on the left opposite the start of the plantation. Look for the signpost on the left by the gate for the Bayr ny Skeddan and this time follow the clearly defined track until you arrive at the gate to the Creg ny Crok plantation.

Cross the stile and walk straight on through the plantation with the pointed top of Slieau Whallian straight ahead in the distance. Look for the signpost and the path going off to the right down through the plantation opposite the ruined building. It is hard to remember that when this collection of walks was first put together in 1989 this whole area was open with all the trees that are here now just starting to grow.

Follow the track between the trees down the side of Dalby Mountain. You are now walking down the west side of Glen Rushen and emerge in the open just before the bottom of the valley. The original raw water intake for the original Peel water supply, which feeds a reservoir further down the valley, is below and on the opposite side of the valley can be seen the surface remains of Beckwiths Mine and its drunken stone chimney.

Join the track in the bottom of the glen, through the gate and walk over the bridge to cross the river and continue down the Glion Mooar *(the great glen),* which is the name given to the whole valley from South Barrule to the sea at Glen Maye. As you continue down the track you will pass some surface remains from Beckwiths mine on the right. The mine is flooded to adit level and the water you see discharging under the track into the river is the overflow from the adit. On the left, pass the reservoir referred to earlier, which is built in one of the old quarries.

As you join the Glen Rushen Road you will pass below the ruins of some miners' cottages up on the right in the trees. The track joins the Glen Rushen Road. Fork left and follow the narrow road down under the trees for about 1km. As you emerge from the

Bethwiths Mine Glen Rushen as seen across the valley from the path

shade of the trees the spoil heaps from the old quarries are clearly visible on the left-hand side of the valley, although most of the old workings are now obscured by forestation.

Look very carefully for the track leading up into the plantation on your right. It climbs steeply away from Glen Rushen Road. Follow it through the gate and into Arrasey Plantation. The plantation track climbs steeply to the top where you should fork right and continue uphill until it levels out below the old Arrasey farm. This is the best place to stop and look across Glen Rushen to the right and view the remains of the old slate quarry.

This is the quarry mentioned in the introduction and where up to 120 men worked at its height of production. There were crude narrow gauge tramways on each of the levels and spoil was pushed manually to the end of each level and tipped down the hillside and the form of these tips can still be determined. The levels were served by inclines.

The track continues around Arrasey Hill with South Barrule ahead and Cross Vein Mine almost on the skyline. On reaching the surfaced road leading to Glen Maye, turn left and walk up the hill (the last one I promise) to the crossroads at the Eairy Ranch. Turn right through the gate and follow the track *(Bayr Glass)* around the side of Slieau Whallian. Soon you will start to descend towards St John's. Stop to look at the view to the right over Foxdale where many of the features described in walk No.8 and the introduction can be seen in context.

At the end of the track join the Gleneedle Road and fork left continuing down to St John's, joining the point where the walk along the Foxdale Line joins the same road to return to St John's.

WALK 18
AGNEASH & CORNAA VALLEY TO RAMSEY

This is a 19km walk. You should allow 7 hours and it is advisable to take refreshments. The walk ends in Ramsey and takes in a number of industrial archaeological sites.

You should get to Laxey to start this walk and what better way to get there than by electric tram. In the summer you can treat yourself to a ride on a horse tram along Douglas Promenade to the Derby Castle terminus of the Manx Electric Railway. Laxey is also served by bus route No.3. Whichever way you get there this walk starts from the tram station at Laxey. It embraces part of Walk No.5 as you leave the village.

Leave the tram station past the Mines Tavern, taking care to look out for the trams. This public house was once the mine captain's house, built overlooking the washing floors of the Great Laxey Mines. Head off along the main road for a short distance before crossing it to walk along Dumbell's Row. To your left you can see the track of the Snaefell Mountain Railway starting its climb to the top of the Island's highest mountain and also the memorial to the miners who died in the Snaefell Mine disaster. Ahead you can see the Great Laxey Wheel as you walk along 'Ham and Egg Terrace'. The terrace of mine workers cottages earned its name from the reputation it had for providing visitors with good meals as they passed this way to see the 'Lady Isabella' at the height of the pre-war tourist boom.

As you pass the fire station look across the river to the bank on the opposite side. There is the entrance to the Cross Cut Adit which was dug in 1868 to connect the Main Adit to the Mines Yard. The changing rooms were adjacent to the tunnel entrance. Continue up the road towards Agneash. Opposite the engineering works is a car park where the lower end of the Browside Tramway was located.

Pass the entrance to the Laxey Mines Trail and rounding the corner you will see the Wheel at the top of the hill straight ahead of you. I always feel that this view shows the true scale of the Wheel as it relates to the houses either side of the road. Turn left before reaching the Wheel and continue uphill to Agneash. After the hairpin corner and as you approach the village you will have a good view to your right of the area of the main mine working. The building seen on the opposite side of the valley is the Engine House which housed a beam engine used for winding the kibble carrying the ore out of the Engine shaft and the Welch shaft, although it is generally thought that the engine was also used for pumping. There is evidence also that a wheel was built on the same site and that the engine house was built around it but industrial archaeologists are excavating to determine more about the precise function of this building, which was central to the heart of the mine.

Coming into Agneash village the hill ahead of you is Slieau Lhean *(Broad mountain)* and to the right Slieau Ouyr *(Brown mountain)*. Deep below the galleries of the Great Laxey Mine stretch under the village. To your right on the opposite hillside north east of the village are the remains of some stone-built buildings which were the head works of Dumbell's shaft. As described in the introduction this was the deepest shaft in the mine, reaching a depth below the adit of 552 metres. Slieau Lhean is 461m above sea level and the adit is about 100m below at Agneash, which gives some idea of the scale of the mine.

With those facts occupying your mind take a left fork by the village green and walk up the north side of the Laxey Valley past Ballayolgane farm, heading for the Great

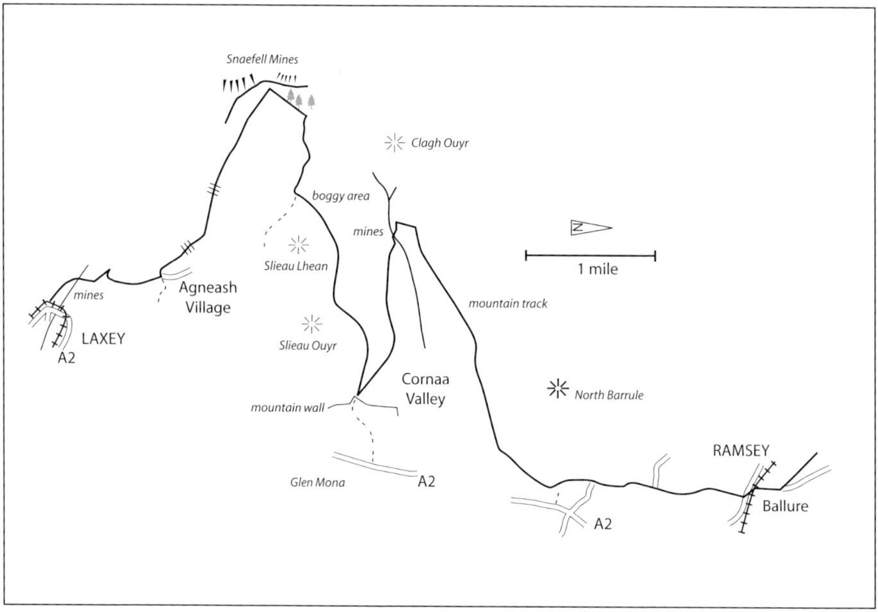

Snaefell Mine which is located at the head of the valley. You can readily appreciate that you are in a classic glacial valley. On the left across the valley the line of the Snaefell Mountain Railway can be seen clinging to the side of Mullagh Ouyr *(dun or brown summit)* as it climbs to the summit of Snaefell *(Snow Mountain)*. At 621m this is the highest mountain on the Island.

The road on which you are walking gradually deteriorates into a stony track and ends at the head of the valley at the site of the mines. Some surface remains exist, including the mine captain's house and a chimney from the original workings. Most of the present surface features, which are brick-built, date from the early 1950s when the spoil heaps were re-worked by a company who were successful in retrieving some valuable metals by modern techniques.

The mine commenced work in 1856 and photographs show a large wheel located across the neck of the glen ahead near the chimney. This is the wheel that has been rebuilt in the wheelcase on the lower washing floors (described in Walk No.5). The mine was driven in a northerly direction for a distance of almost 1km and a much less distance south. There was one shaft, the top of which is visible to your right and surrounded by a substantial masonry wall. The mine was sunk to a depth of 171 fathoms (312m). In May 1897 a disaster occurred at the mine in which twenty men lost their lives due to a fire in the mine at the 130 fathom level which filled the underground workings with poisonous gases. The mine continued working until 1908 and was productive throughout with galena and zinc blende being the principal minerals.

Leaving the mine, follow the signpost beside the mine captain's house up the flank of Clagh Ouyr *(Brown stone)*. The path is obscure and you should use a compass taking a bearing of 45 degrees. If in doubt, just head upwards and as the going levels out you should pick up the line of an old track which you should join and follow to the right in an easterly direction. Before heading off in the new direction just look back and observe the line of the extensive system of water collection which fed the reservoirs across the head of the valley to provide the power for the water-wheel.

You will shortly arrive at a boggy area in the saddle between Clagh Ouyr and Slieau Lhean, through which you will have to pick your way, which is all part of the fun of hill walking. Take care here and make a left turn. There should be a signpost here but it is regularly blown down in winter. Skirt the north side of Slieau Lhean and Slieau Ouyr, following a clearly defined track until you come to the mountain wall, all the time commanding a good view of the North Barrule ridge and North Barrule, whilst straight ahead you can see over the parish of Maughold with Maughold Head and the lighthouse in the distance.

At the mountain wall turn hard left and back-track up the Cornaa valley at a lower level. The track is not defined, it is really another leat for collecting water for more mine workings, but it is easy on a clear day to head up the valley using the clearly pointed outline of Clagh Ouyr as a guide. As the head of the valley comes into view you can see the ruins of North Laxey Mines. Taking care crossing a deep gulley you should now be able to see the line of your route as it follows the old mill race which fed water to a large wheel and the washing floors. The position of the wheel can be clearly seen as you approach the workings where the water was carried across the valley in a timber aqueduct supported on three stone piers.

The remains of the washing floors are quite clearly seen as you drop down to the river which you have to cross, taking care not to get your feet wet. It is not a bad place to stop for it is usually possible to find somewhere out of the wind for a break. The mine was started in the mid part of the nineteenth century. Two shafts were sunk. The

North shaft eventually reached a depth of 174 fathoms and the South shaft 110 fathoms. By 1897 the mine had ceased working and although it had produced 1763 tons of lead ore it never recovered its cost.

Suitably refreshed, strike up the other side of the valley by way of a sheep fold to pick up a clearly defined track which takes you back down the valley below North Barrule, heading for a ruined house in the distance.

The ruin is Park Llewellyn house and as you pass it continue through a gate onto a more clearly defined road between two stone hedges. All the time you are skirting Barrule *(the name is a Norse derivation and is connected with the ancient duty of watch and ward which discontinued in 1815)* and under the stone crags of the east face, frequented by a pair of ravens, you will join a surfaced roadway at Hibernia which you should follow for almost a kilometre, going straight on where the road veers left.

The view over the northern plain shows the fertile land of the northern parishes and the Bride Hills in the distance with just a glimpse of the Point of Ayre lighthouse at the northernmost tip of the Island. Ramsey, your destination, is just below you and you will quickly descend this track, which was the old road from Ramsey to Douglas and which is steep and quite difficult under foot.

Finally, join the present main road to Ramsey at Ballure which you should follow over the tram crossing into the town of Ramsey. If you follow Waterloo Road for about 1½ km you will be at the tram station for your return to Douglas or the alternative of a return trip on the bus. If you have time why not look around Ramsey – see the town walk for Ramsey.

Parliament Street has a good selection of shops and numerous alleys lead off to the harbour, where there is usually plenty to see. Why not visit the Electric Railway Museum, adjacent to Ramsey station, housed in the original running shed. There are a number of interesting exhibits including the former Queens Pier tramway locomotive and train.

The Queens Pier was built in 1886 as a low water landing pier for the town, which was the principal town for the north of the Island. The tramway was built to 3ft gauge and provided a facility originally for hand-propelled luggage trucks. Later, in 1937, a Planet petrol-engined locomotive and a fifteen seat trailer was purchased to carry passengers to the end of the pier. In 1950 an eleven seat Wickham petrol-engined railcar was added to the fleet. The tramway ceased operation in the mid 1970s at which time the Steam Packet Company vessels stopped calling at Ramsey.

North Laxey Mines showing the surface remains

WALK 19
THE HERITAGE TRAIL

This is an 18km walk along the disused railway track-bed between Douglas and Peel. Starting at Douglas Railway Station, leave by the steps under the clock tower, taking time to admire the grandeur of the station buildings and the grand entrance from Athol Street.

When the railway was built in 1873, the Isle of Man Railway Company had a simple wooden building as its station and its offices located in Athol Street, which was then and still is to some extent, the business centre of the town. It was surprising then, for such a small Island, that by 1892 the railway company had risen in stature to build a station which would be the envy of many main line railways, let alone comparable narrow gauge railways. The railway had arrived.

This walk follows the route of the first line to be completed which connected Douglas to Peel. Unfortunately the first half mile or so has been extensively built over so you will have to make a detour before joining the line at the Quarterbridge.

Make your way up Peel Road, passing the shops on the left which were built by the ever-enterprising Railway Company. Follow the road to the junction with Pulrose Road and turn left over the bridge. It is worth stopping to look at this bridge, which was built in 1938 to replace an earlier level crossing. This is the route of the line to follow but you cannot yet join it. You will note that the bridge has two arches making provision for doubling the line, something that never happened. You will also be able to make out the route of the track-bed as it threads its way behind the development of this area which has taken place over the last twenty-five years.

Continue on towards the Power Station and turn right before the bridge over the Douglas River, which you should follow behind the Bowl, part of the King George V playing fields. The whole area was reclaimed using waste from the spoil heaps at Foxdale. No.15 CALEDONIA was almost exclusively used to haul thousands of tons of material here between 1935 and 1939.

The path takes you to the confluence of the River Dhoo (*black river*) and the River Glass (*green river*) and now you can see how the name of the town evolved. Follow the right fork alongside the Glass and cross it by the bridge which leads to the National Sports Centre. Continue following the river for a short distance past the rear of the grandstand and join the railway track behind the office building. This is where the railway crossed the river on a skew lattice girder bridge.

You can start your walk in earnest with a short walk on the old track-bed until you reach the site of the level crossing which carried the railway across the Castletown Road at the Quarterbridge. Note the crossing keeper's gatehouse on the left. Take care crossing the road, visibility is restricted and it is a very busy road.

The next section of the track-bed has been surfaced to allow vehicular access to the inside of the TT course when the main road is closed for motorcycle racing. Continue behind Quarterbridge Lodge and through the gate across the track and walk between the stone boundary walls. On the left you will see Kirby Estate and if you are lucky you may catch sight of grey herons which roost here and range the river. *(The name Kirby is Scandinavian in origin and means Church Farm.)*

As you pass under the road, approach the site of the former Braddan Halt. This was used in connection with open air Sunday services at Braddan Parish Church, which you will shortly just be able to see to the left. It was not uncommon to see ten coach trains on this

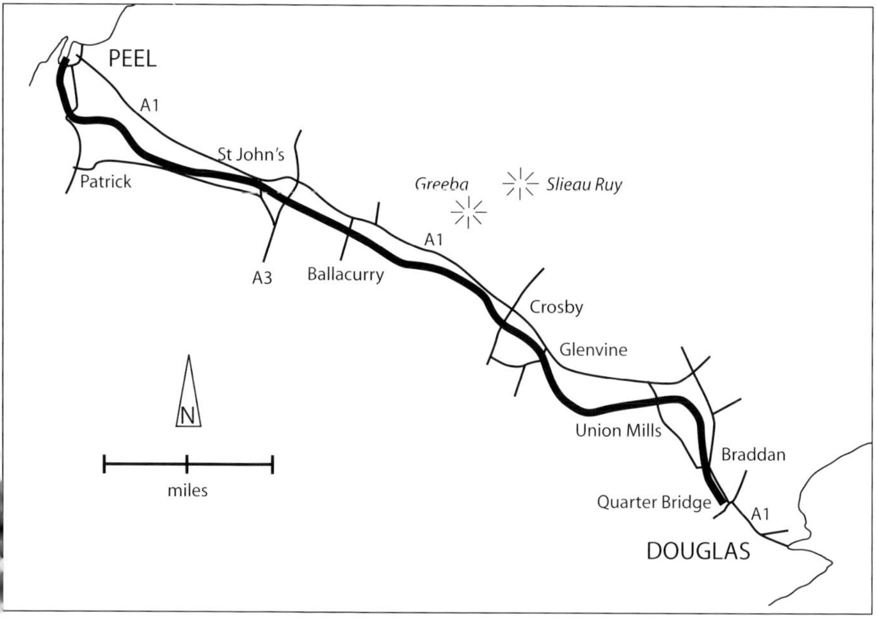

short special service from Douglas and hundreds of visitors getting off the train with no platform and walking up the steps by the bridge and up Vicarage Road to the fields behind the new parish church. For the railway it did result in some interesting positioning movements at Union Mills and special ticket working with more than one train occupying the single track.

You will soon leave the surfaced access road and modern housing development. Carry straight on along the old track-bed now more recognisable as a disused railway. The River Dhoo, which has never been very far away, is now beside the railway. The Local Commissioners have provided a wooden walkway between the railway and the river as part of a conservation scheme.

As you approach Union Mills the line curves left after crossing the river on a steel girder bridge. This replaced an earlier stone-built structure which gave rise to trouble with flooding in the early years of the railway. A small wayside halt existed here at the outset in connection with a horse-racing course at the Strang.

Now with industry left behind, the scenery becomes more pleasant. It is hard to realise that even as late as 1960 there was little or no industrial development between Pulrose Bridge and Union Mills!

Entering Union Mills Station through the tall trees which have grown with the railway you are now 2½ miles from Douglas. Early photographs show almost no cover at all. Successive Station Masters took a tremendous pride in the station which became noted for its wonderful display of rhododendron and floral displays.

The station was on the curve and had a very long passing loop, which was added after 1906. On the left you will see the single platform serving the station. Look for the name of the manufacturer of the non-slip paving slabs which form the edge of the platform. Also on the left before you reach the platform there is a roadway accessing the station area. There was a short trailing siding here serving a cattle dock and for goods traffic. The wooden station building was situated on the right just before the line passed under the road.

Part of the development of the Heritage Trail has been the inclusion of some picnic tables and also descriptive boards. Here at Union Mills a static display has been included. The Gibbins breakdown crane, one of two operated by the IMR, is displayed on a small section of track. Dating from 1893 it was hand operated and had a lifting capacity of 8 tons.

Immediately after crossing the River Dhoo yet again (the original steel structure was removed when the line was being dismantled) continue past a small industrial area where the remaining parts of the old Union Mills *(the name evolved because a corn mill and a woollen mill built on the same site by William Kelly both drew water for their machinery from the same dam)* can still be seen and are still in use as small industrial units. The Mills were a big employer for this area in the early part of the nineteenth century.

Later they were owned by the Dalrymple family, who continued to operate them until the end of the century. Dalrymple Maitland was a director of the railway and locomotive No.11 was named after him.

Cross the Trollaby stream *(possibly the stream of the trolls)* and now enter open country as the line sweeps into the central valley of the Island. The River Dhoo is still on the left and you can see remnants of the curragh *(bog)* between the river and the railway. Much of the central valley was like this, with wet boggy land, water meadows and willow growing in what was in effect the flood plain of the river.

Henry Vignoles, when he surveyed the route for the line, chose a route which skirted the valley floor and just managed to keep above the water table. The line passed Glen Lough *(literally Lake Glen)* and then ran straight for a short distance to cross the road

IMR No 15 Caledonia at Closemooar crossing bound for snow clearing duties in 1964

at Closemooar *(great enclosure)*, just after milepost 4. The crossing keeper's gatehouse still survives and is on the left before the crossing.

There was a short cutting here and then the line ran straight towards Marown Church with Greeba Mountain dominating the view. The track-bed here has also been surfaced to allow access to the nearby sewage works. Be careful of lorries accessing the works.

Pass below the parish church and swing left, entering more curragh land before approaching another road crossing which was controlled by a level crossing, where once again the gatehouse remains.

Cross the road and enter the playing fields. This was the site of Crosby Station, some 4¾ miles from Douglas. Nothing remains to give a clue as to what was here. There was a passing loop and the facing point for this was positioned just before the level crossing and two tracks crossed the road. This meant that when trains passed here the road was obstructed for longer than usual. If the second train was late the gates would often be opened in between the passing operation.

There was a typical IMR wooden station building, painted green and cream, on the right just as you enter the playing fields. And just beyond that a wooden goods shed served by a siding off the passing loop with a further short siding to a cattle dock, the whole of which was partly screened by a wooden boarded fence.

Greeba *(an obscure Scandinavian word meaning peak)* is now much closer and the hills on both sides are closing in on the route that the railway took. You are still climbing and haven't yet reached the summit. On the hill on the left above the Highway Depot you can see the old school which served the Parish of Marown.

Leaving the playing fields you will soon be back on the old track-bed. Straight ahead is Creg y Whuallian *(rock of the whelp)* with Cooillingill Farm *(low nook)* on the hillside. You will just be able to see the edge of Archallagan Plantation to the left on the skyline. The River Dhoo has its source in the centre of the plantation before tumbling down the hill below Cooillingill and joining the Greeba River on your left.

The line swings right as it passes Greeba and Slieau Ruy *(red mountain)* straight ahead. You are into the true remaining curragh of the central valley as you approach and cross the track leading to Cooillingill Farm. This crossing was an accommodation crossing and the gates were always open to the railway. Walk over another short bridge which crosses the Greeba River and continue close under Creg y Whuallian. You are now passing through the narrowest part of the valley and very near to the summit of the line.

The next level crossing over the Rhenny road *(boayl y rhennee - place of the fern)* was also an accommodation crossing. The house with the unusual farm buildings on the right is Northop *(another Scandinavian word meaning north village)*. You will get another chance to look at Greeba before the curragh closes in and you will pass through a very wet area which was the site of an early settlement. Emerge approaching the Ballacurry Road, which again was an unmanned crossing. You will reach the summit of the line at 185ft, just as you cross the small stream after the Ballacurry Road *(Ballacurry meaning marsh farm)*.

This is the site of an accident in 1909 when the locomotive No.2 DERBY, acting as pilot engine on a late train running to Peel, had the misfortune to hit a fallen tree, was completely derailed and fell onto its side in the bog.

Passing through Greeba, the curragh is still visible in places but over the years drainage work and farming activity has reclaimed a large portion of it. The wooded hill ahead is Slieau Whallian, although its true summit is further to your left. The hill dominates St. John's and it is up the flank of that hill that the Foxdale Railway climbed at 1 in 49 to the mines at Foxdale. I mention the fact whilst you are at this point on the Peel line because the Isle of Man railway had a proposal to build a line to Foxdale at one time and their branch would have made off to the left from almost this location, climbing the side of the hill to the left above Kenna *(Aodha's hill - Aodha being a personal name of Irish descent)*. Cross the Kenna Road, which was yet another unmanned accommodation crossing. After a shallow reverse curve under the trees the track runs straight all the way to St. John's.

Now Slieau Whallian is much closer and you can see the gatehouse for the crossing keeper at the Curragh Road level crossing. The track-bed has been surfaced here and an additional road has been built serving an amenity site. Cross the road and the stile onto the right-hand track, which is the original route of the railway, and pass under the bridge which carried the Foxdale railway over the Peel line. The bridge is covered with ivy but you can see the brick arch springing from the stone abutments.

Now you are approaching the site of St. John's station, which grew from a very modest beginning to become the 'Crewe junction' of the Island's railways. I shall describe it as it was in its final form. The line was single passing under the bridge and ran for a short distance parallel to a three-lane carriage shed, steel framed and galvanised sheet clad, on the right. There was a fourth carriage siding in the open on the far side of the shed, known affectionately as the hospital road. For years rare Cleminson 6-wheel coaches of the former Manx Northern Railway languished in the open, before being scrapped when the line closed.

There was a small signal-box near the trees standing in the middle of the grassed area to your right. Here the line split into two each with a passing loop and served by a low single brick high platform in the centre of the two passing loops. This is where the Ramsey line and the Peel line split. There was a brick structure carrying a water tank at each end of the central platform. To the right there were sidings serving a cattle dock, the remains of which can no longer be seen, and also a head shunt to the carriage sidings.

St.Johns was served by a simple wooden station building which was situated on the left near the road. It had a small waiting room ticket office and Station Master's office and this building was retained to the end, despite the relative importance of the station. Now the whole area is hardly recognisable with a new primary school built on the site of the former sand pits and a sheltered housing complex built on the area where the station was situated.

Two lines crossed the road on a gated level crossing with the Peel line on the left and the Ramsey line on the right. To continue you have to make a slight detour from the original route of the line, which cannot be followed alongside the Mart as the bridges have been removed. It is to your advantage, because you cross the road and through the gate leading to the sewage works, to rejoin the track alongside the works. As you walk down the track, look at the interesting red-brick building behind the hedge on your right. Yes, it does look like a station, because that is exactly what it was. It was the terminus of the Foxdale Railway and was a grand building by comparison with the station belonging to the Isle of Man Railway. It was similar in style to the station building at Foxdale. Mr. Crellin, who was the last station master at St John's, lived in the building with his wife and family for many years.

The Foxdale line incidentally crossed under the road before climbing on a curved embankment to cross over the bridge on the approach to St John's station. Why not take a walk up and look over the bridge walls. The formation of the track can still be seen on either side.

As you rejoin the track-bed pass the site of the only turntable on the whole system. It was located roughly where the large gorse bushes are by the wooden shed adjoining the old station. It was installed as late as 1925 by the IMR, having been purchased second-hand from Co. Clare. Although intended to be installed at Douglas for turning locomotives, shortage of space led to it being installed at St. John's. It saw more use turning the ex Manx Northern Railway Cleminson six-wheeled coaches to ensure even weathering of their varnished finish as the line was exposed to salt spray on the section between St German's halt and Kirk Michael.

Passing through the stile, you are back on clear track-bed again. The two lines were still running parallel with the Peel line on the left and the Ramsey line on the right. The Ramsey line started to rise as it approached the two bridges crossing the River Neb at Ballaleece *(Leece's farm)*. The difference in height between the two bridges shows how the Ramsey line was already gaining the height needed to cross the Peel road as it curved away to the right.

The Peel line, meanwhile, makes a gradual descent from the river crossing before levelling out on the floodplain of the Neb *(the meaning of the name of the river is obscure)*. The river still meanders about this ancient flood-plain and it has prescribed a loop around to your left towards the Patrick Road, joining with the Foxdale River since you crossed the bridges at Ballaleece. Now it is back alongside you as you approach Shenharra *(meaning Old Ballaharra and may refer to an ancient earthwork)*.

On the right is the site of the Abbey Brick and Tile works and sand is still being extracted from the old clay pit which was used by the railway company. A narrow gauge tramway crossed the road and along the top of the hedge to the works, all clearly shown on the 1865 Ordnance Survey maps and researched by others.

The river starts another meander away to your left and you approach the cutting at Ballawyllin *(Byllinge's farm)*, which was notorious in winter for collecting snow. The cutting is through the tail of what appears to be a moraine which was deposited at the time of the retreat of the ice sheet that covered the

Isle of Man during the Ice Age.

Through the crossing at Ballawyllin and you can now see the true flood-plain extending out towards Patrick and the full extent of Peel Hill and Corrin's Hill, surmounted by Corrin's tower. Further to the left are the Creggans *(literally rocky place but describing the small rocky outcrop)* forming the southern boundary to Knockaloe *(Caley or Allowe's hill),* the site of a First World War Internment Camp. A branch of the railway was built to serve this camp and you will see where it joined the Peel line shortly.

The line ran straight for a short distance before skirting the sand cliffs of Ballatersen *(part of the old Bishops Barony but literally meaning - farm of the crozier)* now the location of the Peel Golf Course. You will notice that you are also coming across the last remnants of the Curragh and if you are particularly observant will see the remains of some of the drainage channels dug in the 1940s as a winter employment scheme in a further attempt to drain the area.

Now under the sand cliffs on the right again formed at the end of the Ice Age and you are again back in boggy ground which gave the railway a great deal of trouble throughout its life. You can get some idea of the nature of the ground as you pass close under the sand cliffs. The willow catkins are a sight to behold in the Spring and the area abounds with the yellow heads of the wild Iris.

A little further on and the river is back alongside you and slowed by a dam which was built for the Glenfaba Mill *(as is so often the case with place names we find a mixture of English and Manx. It ought to be Myllin Glenfaba meaning - Mill in the glen of the Neb).* The pond is known locally as the 'red dub' and you can see where the mill race was taken off the dam and under the track on its way to the mill. The name for the area, which also gives its name to the weir, is the Congary *(rabbit warren).*

Before you reach the mill cross a small stream by means of a footbridge. Pay particular attention to the widening of the track-bed just after the bridge. This is where the branch railway to Knockaloe Internment camp left the Peel line by means of a trailing point from this direction. You can just make out the line of the branch as it curved round to cross the river on a wooden trestle bridge to climb for a little over a mile at a gradient of 1 in 20 to Patrick Village and Knockaloe.

Next, on your right, you will come to the Glenfaba Mill and some indication of what it was like can be gleaned from the size and shape of the building. The water-wheels remain and the overflow from them discharged under the track into the river, which is back alongside you. In fact the railway occupied the original river bed here and the river was re-aligned at the time of its building.

The railway passed under the Patrick Road and alongside the river which was also diverted here to allow the railway to run through this natural gorge on a gentle curve. This was the scene of an earlier accident in 1874, again involving the ill-fated locomotive No.2 DERBY, when it fell into the river due to the original embankment giving way following heavy rain. It was the first train of the day and although the driver saw that the track had been washed away he was unable to stop. The driver and fireman both fell with the engine but were uninjured, as was the only passenger who fortunately occupied one of the coaches that did not leave the track. The railway was temporarily diverted on a reverse curve to the right, almost on the original line of the river, whilst the present retaining wall was built to retain the original alignment.

Follow the railway through the remaining fields of Glenfaba farm as you enter Peel through the back door, past the site of the old power station on the left. The Total Oils Storage Depot and the new Peel Power Station on the right are new additions. When the railway was running the first buildings encountered were the brick kilns of the

No.8 Fenella and No.5 Mona double heading a Douglas bound train at Ballachurry the summit of the Peel line

Glenfaba Brick Company, with their tall chimneys: brick built, of course, and, dare I say, aesthetically more pleasing than the slip form concrete chimney presently occupying the site.

Straight ahead and on the left-hand side of the track is one the original kipper houses now operated as a working museum and worth a visit. The modern kipper houses are in the fish yard on the right.

The railway finally arrived at Peel Station by a level crossing across Mill Road and onto the station site which had been reclaimed from the harbour bed. The water tank, the station building and goods shed are the only visible remains of the station, with the last two buildings incorporated into the House of Manannan which now occupies the site. Behind the water tank there was a small engine shed and on the right a cattle loading dock and the goods shed which had a loading bay into Mill Road and which can still just be seen. The station ended with four roads and a run round loop served by a long platform, after having undergone several changes throughout its life.

Peel is 11½ miles from Douglas and you will have walked a little more than that. Now an adjournment to the Creek Hotel (originally The Railway Hotel) and well-earned refreshment is the order of the day.

The railway stopped running between Douglas and Peel in 1972, after five years of uncertainty. The rails had been lifted and sold for scrap before the Isle of Man Government stepped in and purchased everything, which fortunately included the Port Erin line which had remained intact, although it had been a close call.

All of the disused railways have been used for service corridors for gas, electricity, main sewer distribution pipes, water and telephones. At the same time they became public rights of way and were gradually improved for walkers. In 1989 the Peel section, which was the most complete, was designated The Heritage Railway Trail. It is now designated as a cycle way.

There is much to see in Peel, which has retained much of its original character, as well as The House of Manannan which is part of The Story of Mann. Refer to the town walk for Peel and if not yet done now is as good a time as any!

WALK 20
THE RAMSEY LINE FROM ST JOHN'S TO RAMSEY

The total length of this walk is 29 km but there are optional breaks at Kirk Michael (12km) and Sulby Glen (20km) where bus transport back to St. John's or Douglas is available.

Take bus No. 5, No. 5c, No. 6 or No. 6a from Douglas to St. John's from where you will commence your walk to Ramsey

SECTION 1: ST JOHN'S TO KIRK MICHAEL

The Manx Northern Railway constructed their line from Ramsey to St John's in 1879 to meet the demands of the population of the Island. The Islanders felt let down by the Isle of Man Railway when they abandoned their plans for a line to Ramsey due to problems raising the necessary capital, as described in the introduction.

The Manx Northern initially had a separate station at St. John's and passengers had to transfer between trains for onward journeys to Douglas and the south. Later, a junction between the two lines was made and it was in this form when the Isle of Man Railway eventually inherited both the Ramsey line and the Foxdale line.

Walk down Station Road, crossing over the line of the Foxdale railway just before the Post Office. Look for the footpath signs indicating the route of the Heritage Trail. On the left is the area (described in Walk No.19) which used to be occupied by the station and your walk starts here. The station had a simple wooden station building, which was situated on the left near the road the site now being occupied by the end houses of the sheltered housing. It had a small waiting room, ticket office and Station Master's office and this building was retained to the end, despite the relative importance of the junction.

Two lines crossed the road on a gated level crossing, with the Peel line on the left and the Ramsey line on the right, and this is the way you will go.

Passing through the stile follow the track-bed. The two lines were still running parallel with the Peel line on the left and the Ramsey line on the right. Observe where the Ramsey line started to rise alongside the Peel line as you approach the two bridges crossing the River Neb at Ballaleece (*Leece's farm*). The difference in height between the two bridges shows how the Ramsey line was already gaining the height needed to cross the Peel road as it swings away to the right.

Although you will be walking along the Ramsey line, you will have to cross the river on the left-hand span which carried the Peel line. Now look for the signpost and gated stile which takes you back onto the Ramsey line. Once up on the embankment, start to climb gradually to the point where the line crossed the main road between Douglas and Peel. The bridge has been removed and you must climb down the side of the embankment to the road. Cross the road with care as visibility is very restricted and traffic fast. Then go through the stile opposite to rejoin the track-bed.

From this elevated position you will command a good view to the right, down the central valley with the Beary mountain (*Beary being a Scandanavian word meaning 'farm of the sheiling'*) and Greeba (*another Scandinavian word*

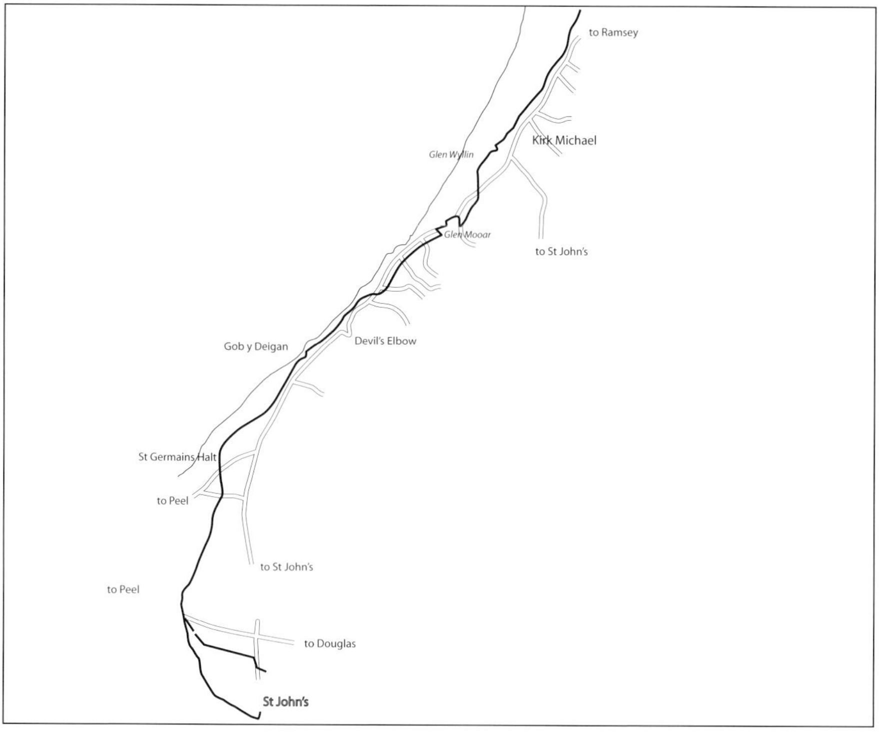

meaning peak) clearly visible. To the left you can see Corrins Hill and Peel Hill. Behind you is the bulk of Slieau Whallian, which is surrounded in folklore.

Tradition has it that if a woman was accused of witchcraft she would be put in a barrel full of spikes and rolled down the hill. If at the bottom she was found to be alive then she would clearly have been a witch and accordingly killed! Seems like rough justice to me.

If you look closely on the right you will see some rolling hills, which are possibly glacial deposits from the melt water of the retreating ice sheet in the Ice Age. Remember that the Island was virtually completely covered during that period. The Island's hills are all rounded by glacial action. The line climbs almost continuously to St. Germans, with some gradients as steep as 1:132. Imagine No.15 CALEDONIA working hard up this climb with a rake of trucks carrying lead or zinc ore from the Foxdale mines.

The line passes through a shallow cutting, after which on the right you will see Poortown Quarry from which almost all the Island's road making stone is won from a granite intrusion. It has been continuously worked since the middle of the nineteenth century. On the left is Cronk ny Lheannagh (*hill of the meadow*), another granite boss with its distinct shape giving the clue to its igneous origins.

You are now approaching a road overbridge at Poortown (*from a personal name - De la Poer*) and the site of Poortown Halt. It was served by an unpretentious timber-framed building situated on the left on the raised concrete platform which can still be seen. The halt was a later addition by the MNR to serve Peel more conveniently than the grand facilities at St. Germans which was their original station for Peel.

Of greater interest are the visible remains on the other side of the bridge. Look to the right as you emerge from the bridge and look at the stone-built wall sloping down to a loading bay. You might still be able to see the remains of some sleepers on top of it if you scratch through the briars. A 2 ft gauge tramway ran down the side of the public road from Poortown Quarry and into this loading bay which was served by a siding.

The stone was loaded at the quarry into 'jubilee trucks' which ran mostly by gravity to the station and then hauled back by horse. The horse was kept in a stable next to the compressor house - and no I can't remember the name of the horse although I was told its name years ago by one of the men who had worked with the horse! The Highway Board moved stone from Poortown Quarry to its parish depots in this manner for many years.

The line curves to the right under the flank of Knocksharry (*derived again from a personal name and literally means McSharrey's hill*) with views towards Peel on the left. The next bridge that you approach is a plate girder bridge similar to Poortown, which carries the East Lhergydhoo road over the railway. After the next cutting pass under the Lhergydhoo (*black slope*) road. It is carried on one of the more usual stone-built arched bridges with dressed corner stones, which typified the civil engineering work on the MNR.

Emerge on a curved embankment to approach St.Germans station and the level crossing over the Peel/Kirk Michael road almost at milepost 3. Despite some quite recent changes, the layout of the station can still be seen together with the station and gatehouse. There was a passing loop and goods siding here. It is hard to believe that the station was originally built to serve Peel some 2 miles away! Imagine getting off the train in the winter, having been to Ramsey, to be faced with a walk back home in a gale of wind and pouring rain.

Leaving the station area on the curve below Knocksharry farm emerge on an exposed part of the west coast of the Island. It was a bleak place to work as a lengthman in winter when this whole section was subject to snow, particularly when it came from the south east, despite being in the rain shadow area of

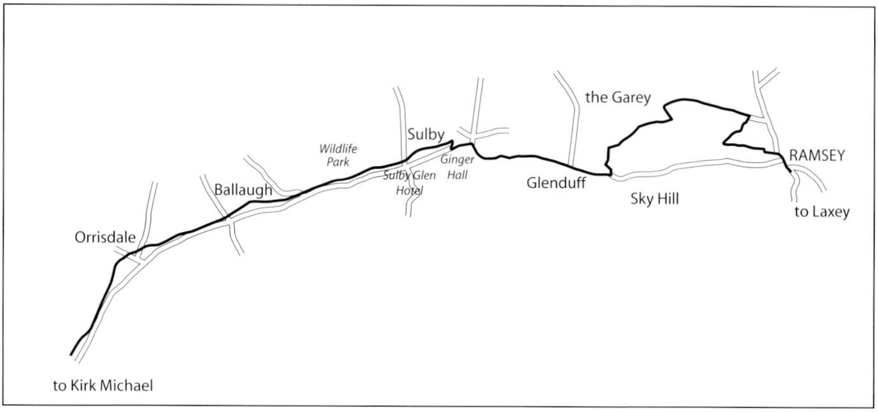

the adjoining hills.

The line crosses a number of deep glens between here and Kirk Michael. The first is Glen Broigh *(dirty glen probably associated with Glion Mucklagh - meaning pigstye glen - a side glen which drains into Glion Broigh)* which is crossed on a high earth embankment. This steep-sided wooded glen and its unusual mix of trees and palms can only really be appreciated from the railway. The formation continues to climb ahead of you towards Lynauge and Gob y Deigan and you can just make out the cut in the outline of the hill ahead where the line emerges onto the cliff.

Approach a stone-arched overbridge at Lynauge (*heather creek derived from the Scandinavian Lyngvik*) and pass through the cutting that you could see in the distance. Now you suddenly emerge onto the embankment above the sandy shore at Lynague, although often referred to as Gob y Deigan, from the adjacent headland. Imagine how dramatic it was sitting in a coach on the train looking out at the grass side of the cutting and then the next minute nothing but sea and sky! Memories of travelling by train on Sunday School picnics to Glen Wyllin always come back to me here. As a small boy I could barely see out of the window and when there was nothing but sea out of the window it seemed like the end of the world had arrived.

It was not so romantic for the MNR and later the IMR. This ledge and the next embankment, often referred to as the 'donkey bank', were nothing but a headache for the railway companies. They were subject to constant movement and settlement, being constructed on sandy cliffs. The effects can be clearly seen as you walk over the track-bed. If you look in through the trees on the right you might just be able to see some of the large earthenware pipes which were put in many years ago in an attempt to improve the drainage.

As you enter the next cutting the remains of the plate-layers' hut can be seen on the left. The next section was also problematical with flooding and you may have to pick your way through as you approach Ballakaighen farm.

Now cross Glion Cam (*the winding glen*) which is the next major obstacle. Here the railway crossed the glen on another high embankment, with dramatic views on both sides. The coast road is still close to the railway and it can be seen to the right snaking round the head of the glen at the Devil's Elbow.

The railway entered a cutting here and curved inland to cross under the road, which was originally carried over on a skew bridge at Skerisdale (*yet another Scandinavian derivative from Skeresstaor meaning rock farm*). The bridge has recently been changed to an embankment with a tunnel under the embankment for the use of walkers. Emerge in a rock cutting and pass Ballaquine farm and the summit of the line 5 miles from St. John's.

You now command a view of the west coast, with Kirk Michael in the middle distance and Jurby Head as far north as you can see. The sand cliffs are all too apparent and the proximity of the erosion is now putting the coast road itself under threat. Cross a number of farm crossings before coming to Glen Mooar (*big glen*). The railway crossed this glen on three lattice girder spans carried on two masonry piers. You will have to climb down the side of the abutment and past one of the piers. Stop and look up and you will get some impression of what it was like to cross this glen on the railway.

Because the spans have been removed, you will have to make a considerable detour as there is no way up the other side of the glen to rejoin the track. Follow the path through the glen to the coast road, turn right and walk up the hill to the next junction. Turn right again up the Ballaleigh road, looking out for the level crossing. The gatehouse on the right, although modernised, still retains its hipped gables and is a good clue. Turn left to rejoin the track-bed which runs through a cutting at West Berk (*a quarterland name again of Scandinavian origin from Borgarvik meaning creek of the fort*). This was another place susceptible to filling with snow.

Caledonia charging a snow drift at Skerisdale

No15 CALEDONIA ran off the rails here charging snowdrifts in 1965.

Under the road again and into what can be a very lovely part of the whole line. Imagine one of the MNR Sharp Stewart 2-4-0s steaming briskly chimney first towards you under the arch of the bridge carrying the accommodation road at Ballacregga (*rock farm - this time from the Manx but more correctly Balley ny creggey*).

Curving round in the cutting the railway came to the last of its major obstacles Glen Wyllin (*mill glen*). It was crossed on another three span girder bridge at a height of almost 60ft from the valley floor. Again the steelwork has been removed so you have no alternative but to take the path down the side of the abutment into the glen, cross the river and climb up the zig-zag path on the other side to reach the station at Kirk Michael 7¼ miles from St. John's.

The station and goods shed still remain and have been put to good use within the local community. The goods shed is now the fire station for the area and houses two modern appliances.

Kirk Michael is a good place for a lunch stop and facilities exist in the village up Station Road. If you only intend doing the first section of the walk then public transport from the village by bus using No. 5, No. 5c or No. 6 will get you back to St. John's or Douglas.

SECTION 2: KIRK MICHAEL TO SULBY

The railway left Kirk Michael on a raised embankment running straight for a mile. In the distance you will just be able to see the line disappear under a bridge. To the right is the village and also the Parish Church which was built in 1835. The western hills form an impressive backdrop. From right to left they are Sartfell (*Scandinavian - black hill*), Slieau Freoaghane (*bilberry mountain*) and Slieau Curn (*taking its name from an early Irish personal name - McCurry*). You now have some easy walking ahead as the line is generally downhill all the way to Ramsey.

Cross over the Balleira Road (*a mixture of Manx and Scandinavian Balley and Leir· meaning place of the muddy river*) on a plate girder bridge, which gave the MNR trouble with movement on one of the abutments, requiring an elaborate buttress to be built over the stream. Soon you will reach the bridge that you could see as you left the station, the first of three stone-built arched bridges carrying roads over the railway.

Walk through the deep cutting at Rhencullin (*holly ridge*), which was another snow trap in winter, then onto a shallow embankment sweeping round behind Bishopscourt. It is now a private residence but formerly was the seat of the Bishop of Sodor and Mann from its inception in the 13th century until recent times. There was a request halt for Bishopscourt, which was no more than a wooden bench situated where the public right of way to Orrisdale *(Scandinavian Orrastaor - moorfowl estate*) crosses the track.

The trains used to get a fair old rattle on here as they approached the level crossing at Orrisdale No.1. Then through the cutting on the curve to a second level crossing at Orrisdale No.2 where the Bollagh Jiarg (*the red road - more recently referred to as the Bollyn Road*) was crossed. Both of these crossings were protected by signals as the crossings were unsighted and the drivers would not have been able to see the normal hand signal from the gatekeeper.

Now you are on to a long straight section to Ballaugh: in fact one of the features of the line from here to Ramsey was its long straight sections. You are close to the main road to Ramsey now and shortly will pass the Bishop's Dub. This is a small pond which sometimes dries in summer but if you are lucky you may see some wading birds, swans or, more likely, coots.

You have passed Slieau Curn and are now close under Ballaugh Mountain (*Ballaugh is the name for the village and also the parish. It has been corrupted from the Manx Balley ny Loghey place of the lake*) as you skirt some of the sand hills at Brough Jiarg (*red brow or hill*) before crossing the farm access road. Cross Ballaugh River on a small plate girder bridge and then the Ballaugh Coast Road before entering the area formerly occupied by Ballaugh station. You are now 10 miles from St. John's.

The station area has been opened up and made into an amenity area. Very little is left to give a clue as to what was here. There was a passing loop, the facing point for which was immediately before the road, and two tracks crossed the road - as was the case at Kirk Michael. The station building was on the right and the goods shed, which still remains, is on the left. The siding which served that also served a cattle loading dock, which can still be seen.

Leaving Ballaugh, you are really in open country as you curve to the right approaching Ballacrye (*personal name - McCray's farm*) farm and the road crossing with its gatehouse. Look behind and you will see the new Parish Church of St. Mary de Ballaugh which was built in 1832, its unusual pinnacled tower a prominent landmark in the surrounding plain. The extensive northern plain was formed from glacial deposits as the melt water from the retreating ice sheet deposited all its detritus in the area.

Through a shallow cutting approach Ballavolley (*Balley yn vollee - farm of the road*). Look up to the right and you will see the northern slopes of Mount Karrin (*St. Ciarin's mount*) and the remains of several quarries. These were served by a siding adjacent to the railway, the route of which can just be seen as you approach the gatehouse to the road crossing that led into the curragh.

The line was straight for about 2½ miles here and despite the apparent flat appearance there is an uphill gradient towards Ramsey, as anyone who visited the Wildlife Park in the last years of operation of the railway would testify. Trains would often struggle to start away for the next stop at Sulby Glen Station. The park was built within the largest remaining curragh in the Island and you will walk along the edge of it. Cross a minor road level crossing at Cooilbane (*literally white corner*) before approaching Sulby Glen Station, now altered and occupied as a private residence, with traces of the goods loading bay in the garden. The proximity of the station building to the line belies the fact that this was originally a gatehouse which was later converted to a station.

For anyone who has had enough by now, walk off to the right to the main road and buses can be taken to Douglas or Ramsey from the stop outside the Sulby Glen Hotel, where refreshment is available.

SECTION 3: SULBY TO RAMSEY

Cross the road and enter the northern plain with the line running across the flood plain of the Sulby River, which is now to your right and not crossed by the railway for another 2 miles. There is a magnificent view up the Sulby valley to the right, flanked by Mount Karrin (*also sometimes known as the black mountain*) on the right and Slieau Managh (*Slieau ny Maynagh - mountain of the monks part of the Abbeylands*) on the left. Imagine the power generated by the retreating ice sheet in the formative years of the Island. The hills were ground to their present rounded profile and the debris carried by the ice sheet was washed down to form the plains to your left. In the process, the Sulby River, the largest in the Island, meandered about the plain, eventually settling on its present course.

13 miles from St. John's you approach the Kella crossing gatehouse. (*Kella is derived from the Irish Gaelic meaning an island. This has to be seen in the context of the many lakes which once covered the northern plain*). This effectively marks the limit of the track-bed on which you can walk as the remainder is largely in private ownership.

The formation tantalisingly carries on between the hedges to the sandstone-built Sulby Bridge Station, just a short distance away.

However, you must turn right along the Kella Road into Sulby Village and then left to Sulby Bridge, following the main road over the bridge towards the Ginger Hall Hotel, and continue to Ramsey, picking up the old line here and there as you go. Continue up the Ginger Hill crossing from one side of the road to the other to follow the footway. At the top of the hill the road skirts a bluff, hard to discern, formed by the Sulby River on one of its ancient meanders. Drop to Kerrowmooar (*meaning great quarterland*) passing the old chapel and follow the TT course for a mile and a half before turning left at the small road junction to the Garey. Be aware that this section of the walk is not available when the road is closed on certain days for motorcycle racing in June and September.

Follow the road to the Sulby River at Loughan y Yeigh (*pond of the geese*) which you should cross by the footbridge and continue towards the Garey (*rough land*). Look out for the small group of houses on the left and you will see the track-bed running behind them and crossing the road on an angle. Also, on the left is the remains of Lezayre Halt, which was another small station serving the rural community but now converted to a private dwelling.

Carry on to the Jurby Road, turning right towards Ramsey for a little over a kilometre. Look for Gardeners Lane on the right and follow this down to the Sulby River once again. The river is tidal at this point and was in Viking times a sheltered landing place. Cross by the footbridge, known as the white-bridge, following Gardeners Lane for ½km looking for the place where the railway crossed the road at Milntown crossing. The clue again is a converted gatehouse with its hipped gables. Turn left through the gate and join the old railway again for the last kilometre into Ramsey and the site of the station. Little remains to show what it was like as it is now an industrial estate.

Emerging onto Station Road, cross the car park through Parliament Square and follow Queens Pier Road for a short distance to the bus station and transport to Douglas.

WALK 21
BAYR NY SKEDDAN

A 23km walk with good eating facilities at several locations along the way. It takes in a number of industrial archaeological sites and includes some other historic sites touched on in some of the other walks.

The Bayr ny Skeddan is, as the name implies, based on an ancient herring road and as with all the long-distance paths in the Island, a few liberties have been taken along the way.

This path was also introduced in Heritage Year and like the Coastal Path starts at the old water tank at the former railway station at Peel and in fact takes the same route as the coastal path as far as Glen Maye. At Glen Maye as you round the headland, walk up the glen, as described in section one of the Coastal Path, and join the main road at the Waterfall Hotel. Turn right and walk right to the bottom of the hill and left along the Sound Road, as in Walk No.17. Be careful here in the old part of Glen Maye to turn left after a short distance to follow the signpost pointing to the river and the Bayr ny Skeddan. Cross the river on the footbridge and follow the postman's path and climb up the opposite side of the river to join the Glen Rushen Road, now closed to traffic because of a landslip, which you should cross with care and continue up the valley on the old road. If you look across the river and up on the side of Dalby Mountain, you can see

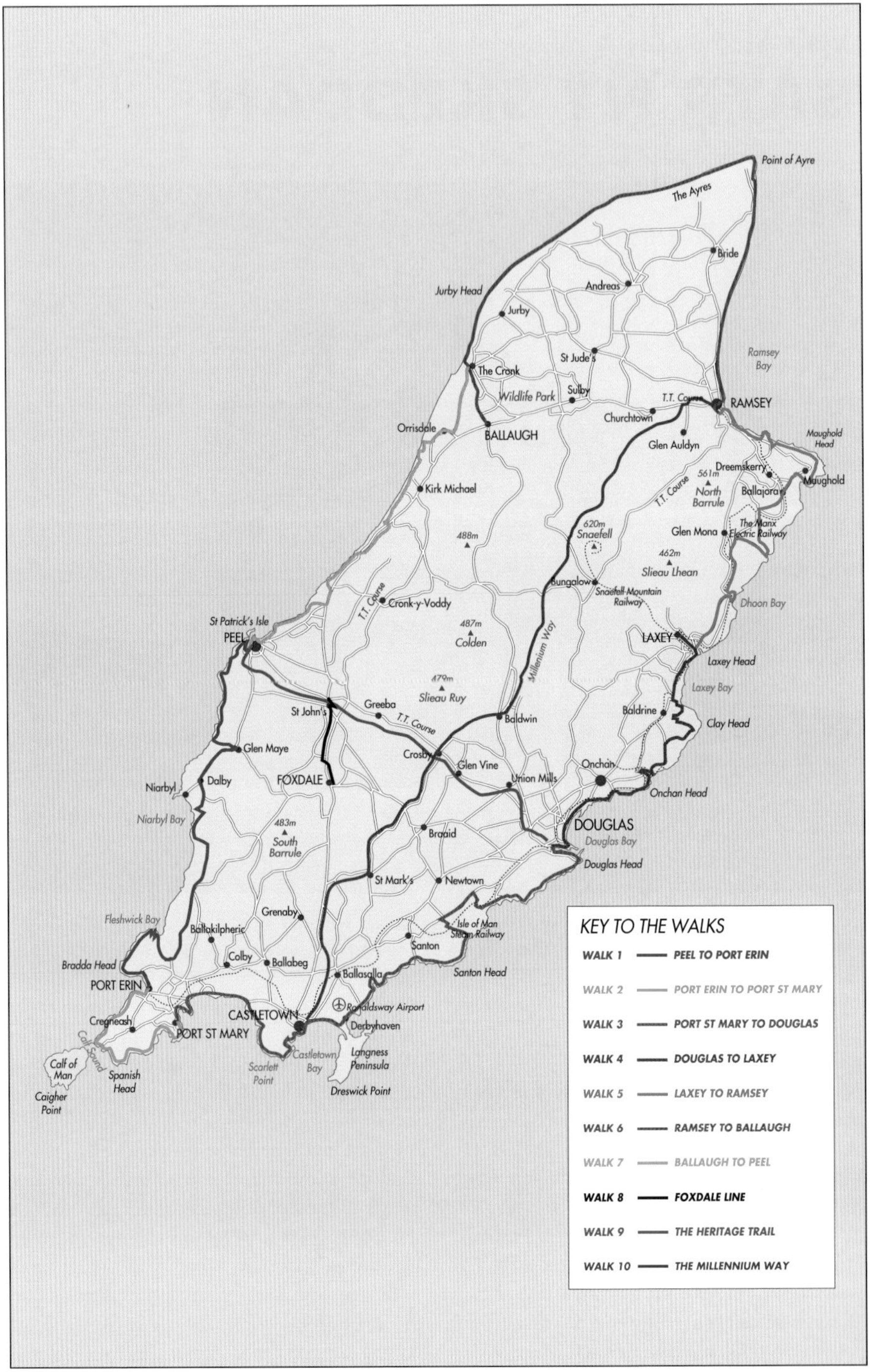
Point of Ayre
The Ayres
Bride
Andreas
Jurby Head
Jurby
St Jude's
Ramsey Bay
The Cronk
Wildlife Park
Sulby
T.T. Course
RAMSEY
Churchtown
Orrisdale
BALLAUGH
Glen Auldyn
Maughold Head
Dreemskerry
561m
North Barrule
Maughold
Ballajora
Kirk Michael
T.T. Course
620m
Snaefell
Glen Mona
The Manx Electric Railway
488m
462m
Slieau Lhean
Bungalow
Snaefell Mountain Railway
T.T. Course
Cronk-y-Voddy
Dhoon Bay
St Patrick's Isle
PEEL
487m
Colden
Millenium Way
LAXEY
Laxey Head
479m
Slieau Ruy
Laxey Bay
St John's
Greeba
T.T. Course
Baldwin
Baldrine
Clay Head
Glen Maye
Crosby
Glen Vine
Onchan
Niarbyl
Dalby
FOXDALE
Union Mills
Onchan Head
Niarbyl Bay
483m
South Barrule
Braaid
DOUGLAS
Douglas Bay
Douglas Head
St Mark's
Newtown
Fleshwick Bay
Grenaby
Ballakilpheric
Isle of Man Steam Railway
Santon
Bradda Head
Colby
Ballabeg
Santon Head
PORT ERIN
Ballasalla
Ronaldsway Airport
Cregneash
CASTLETOWN
Derbyhaven
PORT ST MARY
Calf Sound
Calf of Man
Spanish Head
Castletown Bay
Scarlett Point
Langness Peninsula
Caigher Point
Dreswick Point
KEY TO THE WALKS
WALK 1 PEEL TO PORT ERIN
WALK 2 PORT ERIN TO PORT ST MARY
WALK 3 PORT ST MARY TO DOUGLAS
WALK 4 DOUGLAS TO LAXEY
WALK 5 LAXEY TO RAMSEY
WALK 6 RAMSEY TO BALLAUGH
WALK 7 BALLAUGH TO PEEL
WALK 8 FOXDALE LINE
WALK 9 THE HERITAGE TRAIL
WALK 10 THE MILLENNIUM WAY

clearly the levels of the Glen Rushen Slate Quarries, which were described earlier. Pause and consider the exposed conditions in which the 120 men employed here had to work.

After a short distance, emerge from the tree cover and take a right fork, passing some ruined cottages on the left connected with the Glen Rushen mines, which are now on the hill above you. Continue up the valley alongside the Glen Rushen river until you arrive at a bridge crossing the river and come to some water head works at the end of the road.

Here, follow the waymarkers through the gate on the right and walk up the hillside below the plantation. The path crosses the fence into the plantation a little way up the hill and this is the place to stop and look back down the valley. Ahead of you on the opposite hill you can see the surface remains of Beckwiths mine with its crooked chimney and engine house. In the distance on the skyline is the engine house and chimney of 'snuff the wind', which was Cross Mine, both of which are described in the introduction and Walk No.17 which is walked in the opposite direction. The path is clearly followed through a plantation road on Dalby Mountain and you eventually reach the main road which is followed to the left for approx. 1½ km. to the Round Table crossroads.

Straight ahead is South Barrule *(the word Barrule is derived from the Scandinavian word Vovoufjall meaning ward mountain. It was one of the hills used for watch and ward)*. On a clear day it is worth a short detour to the top to enjoy the magnificent views of the south of the Island. On the way back down there are good views to be had over Cronk Fedjag *(hill of the plover)* and Cronk ny Arree Laa.

However, you must press on straight over the cross roads and after a very short distance take the track to the left. Now you really are on the old herring road leading to Castletown from Dalby used by fishermen taking their catch overland to the capital for sale. You might well ask why the fishermen carried their catch all this way to Castletown. Well Castletown was at that time the capital of the Island and the best prices were to be had there. Also they fished from very small boats entirely dependent on wind and oars for power. The herring were first caught at the start of the season off the west coast of the Island so getting the fish to market by road was not so silly, considering the problems of beating your way at the whim of the wind round to the south of the Island. There was no harbour at Dalby but the boats were hauled up onto the grass sward above Traie Vane, which was a good safe landing-place.

On your right you can glimpse now and again the Cringle Reservoir supplying water to the south of the island. At the next crossroads the Bayr ny Skeddan turns left and leaves the ancient route of the herring road again. I suspect that this has been done to avoid the monotony of walking too far on surfaced roadways.

Follow the route-markers along the Corlea Road and then to the right off the road and down through Glion Cam *(the winding glen)* taking care not to lose your way at the farm at Glen Mooar. The going can be muddy in this area at all times of the year so you will have to pick your way until the track becomes more distinct. Cross the Awin ny Reash *(river of the moor)* and join a surfaced track which you should follow to the main road at the Ballamodha Straight where you will join the Millennium Way to Castletown, as described in walk No.22.

WALK 22
MILLENNIUM WAY

This can be undertaken as a full day walk or as two walks with the break at Crosby. The full length of the walk is about 35km. and Crosby is roughly the half-way point.

The Millennium Way was the first long distance path to be introduced in the Isle of Man as part of the celebrations associated with one thousand years of independent Government. Opened in Easter 1979 it was based on the ancient ridgeway used by the Norse Kings from their ancient landing place on the Sulby River near Skyhill to travel to their fortress on the southern plain. The road is recorded in the Cronica Regum Mannie et Insularum (the Chronicles of the Kings of Man and the Isles) which was the first written record of events within the island and kept by the monks of Rushen Abbey.

Take public transport, either tram or bus, (No. 5, No. 6, No. 6a or No. 5c) to Ramsey and make your way from the tram station to the harbour - a short distance along Parliament Street and down Post Office Lane, which is a narrow cut between the properties opposite the Courthouse. Turn left at the harbour and follow it to the junction with Bowring Road. Note the shipyard on the opposite side of the harbour which was built on the site of a former salt works.

Cross the road at the top of the harbour and look for the public footpath sign leading to Pooyldhooie *(pool of the black ford)* where a nature reserve has been constructed on what used to be the town tip! It is now a very pleasant walk and a credit to the local Commissioners and the volunteers who have carried out the work.

The path emerges by the Whitebridge which crosses the Sulby River and this must have been the most likely place for the Vikings to have made their safe harbour. At the time of their invasions and subsequent settlement the island was a far different place and the Sulby River was by far the biggest river and here they could sail their longships at least a mile and a half from the open sea and moor them in a sheltered lagoon, something which was not possible anywhere else on the Island.

The Norse divided the Island with settlements on the fertile northern plain and the southern plain. To travel between the two, the Kings of Mann used the 'regiam viam' (the king's road) described in the Chronicles. It is the oldest record of any road in the Island and is the route that the Millennium Way generally follows.

Walk up Gardeners Lane to the main road and turn right for a short distance, looking for the distinctive waymarkers for the Millennium Way, striking off to the left over the bulk of Skyhill *(the Norse named it Skogarfjall - the wooded hill)*. Follow the path up through the plantation which was the site of a battle in 1079 when Godred Crovan overcame the native Manx and assumed kingship of the Island.

On leaving the plantation the track opens out on the level near some rugged flat-topped pine trees at Park ny Earkan *(pasture of the lapwing)*. Stop and look back over the northern plain formed by the outwash from the retreating ice sheet which covered the island during the Ice Age towards the Point of Ayre in the far distance.

Carry on to the top mountain gate and enter the open moorland. The track is still discernible and there are waymarkers which you will follow to a very wet boggy area. Cross by means of the planked walkway provided and be careful to follow the waymarkers veering off to the right heading for a cairn on the skyline in the saddle between Slieau Managh *(mountain of the Monks)* and Snaefell *(snow mountain)*.

The 'regiam viam' veered off to the left here and followed more or less the line of the present mountain road for some distance travelling around the east flank of Snaefell. The Millennium Way favours the west flank to keep away from the traffic on the mountain road and at the same time introduces the walker to some of the more inaccessible places in the island.

Pass the cairn and carry on over the saddle a short distance to join the mountain wall above Block Eary reservoir *(from blakkarg meaning black shieling)*. Follow the mountain wall as it turns steeply down below the massive bulk of Snaefell. Cross the wall at the bottom by the stile and over the river.

The way strikes off steeply from the river and at right angles to it. It can be wet here at all times of the year but it is only for a short distance. As you climb it is worth looking back across the valley at the route you have just walked. You should just be able to make out the shape of some circular mounds. These are the shielings where the young men used to live with their animals on the mountain pasture during the summer months. This is a remnant of a past way of life and the best example of its kind on the Island.

Follow the waymarkers across the mountain which run straight over the shoulder of Snaefell until you pick up a stone wall and sod dyke which is part of a large earthwork known as Cleigh yn Arragh *(stone rampart)*. It is easy to lose the route here, particularly in misty weather, and avoid the tendency to veer downhill.

Follow the stone wall and gully until you reach a Forestry Department track which leads to the Tholt y Will Road. Cross the road at the signpost and strike diagonally down the mountain side heading towards the mountain ahead which is Beinn y Phott *(very loosely interpreted as turf peak).* At the bottom of the valley cross the river by means of an old stone bridge which was built and used by the miners who operated the mine which is upstream a short distance. The stone structure that you can see is the remains of the wheelcase of the water-wheel used in connection with the mine which was closed in 1867.

Climb up on the left-hand bank of the gulley ahead being careful at the top to take the left-hand fork - if you don't you will find a nasty bog left from an old turbiary. Aim for the signpost which you should be able to see on the Brandywell Road. This is where the Millennium Way joins the route of the old 'regiam viam' again.

Cross the road and follow the track over the saddle between Beinn y Phott and Carraghyn *(meaning scabby with reference to its stoney top)* as far as the mountain gate, which gives access to a rough track which you should follow for almost 3km. The views open up over the Baldwins and on towards Douglas in the distance as you skirt the shoulder of Carraghyn.

The track starts to drop down at Cronk Keeil Abban *(the hill of St.Abban's church)* where an old keeil was located near an ancient Tynwald site, which is on your right. At St. Luke's Church, which was built as a chapel of ease to Kirk Braddan, you should follow the surfaced road straight ahead taking you downhill into West Baldwin.

At West Baldwin cross the bridge and the road to follow the signs up a track through Ballagrawe *(Balla ny Groa farm of the cotes or coops)* and across the fields of Ballalough *(farm of the lakes).* After passing the farm there is a stone stile which you should cross and turn right into a lane for a short distance before crossing a ladder stile to follow the waymarkers across two fields on the eastern flank of Greeba.

There are superb views to the left over Douglas as you head for the saddle between Greeba and Cronk ny Moghlane or Mucaillyn *(hill of the sows)* and the signpost on the skyline. After the next stile there is a diversion around the edge of the field before reaching the narrow road leading to Cronk Brec *(hill of many colours literally piebald).* You must now make a left and right turn to follow a rough stone track down to Ballaharry. Just before you reach the cottages, look to the right and the sign pointing to an ancient monument. This is the site of the remains of Keeil Vreshey *(the church of St. Bridget)* and is an example of early Celtic Christianity, of which there were many such sites.

At Ballaharry the track joins a surfaced road which will take you into Crosby village at the crossroads with the main Douglas to Peel highway. Here you can finish the walk and return to Douglas by public transport or if you are really energetic you can carry on with the southern section of the walk to Castletown.

The southern section of the Millennium Way is totally different in character and the old 'regiam viam' would have passed to your left to cross between the Mount and Slieau Chiarn *(the Lord's mountain)* and has been incorporated into the present road network. In order to keep the Millennium Way more attractive to walkers it takes a slightly different but parallel route.

If you are just starting or if you have stopped at the local hostelry for lunch, then it is a tough start. Make your way down Old School Road past the Memorial Playing Fields and cross the old railway track. Then it is a stiff climb up School Hill, passing the old school which was built in 1874. Its bleak location may seem a little strange when you look around and see where the centre of population is now. When it was built, however, the school was in the centre of the parish, serving numerous remote farmsteads as well as the village.

The same factors applied to the old parish church which you will pass at the top of the hill. The church is dedicated to St.Runius and dates from the 12th century, although there is a record of an earlier keeil on the site, dating from the 7th century, the remains of which can be seen in the church grounds.

Continue along the road under the avenue of trees towards the Garth crossroads. Look out for the ancient monument sign on the right as you start to climb the next hill. It directs you to the site of St. Patrick's Chair, which is a small group of stones where tradition has it that this is the spot where he first preached to the nation, introducing Christianity to the Kingdom of Mann.

Carry straight on over the crossroads passing Ballanicholas and drop down the hill to Campbells Bridge, marking the boundary between the parishes of Marown and Malew. Stop at the bridge which spans the Santon River to read the interesting plaque on the bridge and if you look over the bridge you may just be able to make out the remains of some mine workings.

Continue on past Shenvalley *(old farm)* and in the distance you will be able to see the tower of the church at St. Marks. The church is a good landmark and you must turn right and then left at St. Marks around the old schoolhouse. The church, school and adjoining houses were built in the 18th Century at the instigation of Bishop Hildesley. The church was built as a chapel of ease to Malew parish church.

You need to be careful here and look for the waymarker beside the old parsonage. The path follows the lane beside the parsonage to the Awin Ruy *(red river)* which is crossed on an old stone slab. The path meanders through the fields of Upper and Lower Ballagarey *(farm of the river thicket),* crossing hedges through kissing gates, eventually arriving at a surfaced road.

Cross the road and follow the waymarkers through two fields before entering Ballamodha Mooar farm yard and following the farm road through Ballamodha Beg to its junction with the Ballamodha Road *(Ballamodha meaning farm of the dogs and Mooar meaning big and Beg little).*

Turn left and walk along the road for approximately 1½ km, taking care as there is no footpath. The Ballamodha straight has been used in the past for motor-car hill climbs and reliability trials when the motor-

Crossing the stream at the foot of Beinn y Phoot

The ancient Tynwald site at Cronk y Keeill Abban

car was in its infancy.

Continue to the bottom of Silverburn hill and at the Atholl Bridge turn left into Silverdale and walk on a riverbank path alongside the river. Approaching Silverdale you will walk into a children's playground, boating lake and café. The boating lake gives the clue to the function of the old building adjoining the café which was the Creg Mill, one of two built by the Monks of Rushen Abbey. The boating lake was the dam providing the power for the mill wheel. The little water-wheel which powers the children's roundabout is worth more than a passing glance as it came from the Foxdale Mines when they closed.

Continuing downstream, pass the site of more industry from the past where Ballasalla Ochre and Umber Works were located and it is now converted into a private residence. The company was a substantial one and had warehousing in Castletown from where their shipments were made. The north quay still carries the name Umber Quay, a reminder of the past activity.

Leaving the wooded glen you emerge through a gate at Monk's Bridge, which is probably the oldest bridge in the Island dating from the late 13th/early 14th century and built by the Monks of Rushen Abbey.

As you approach the site of the Abbey look to the left on the opposite side of the river for the Abbey Mill, which is now converted to private apartments. It was a substantial mill and had an internal water-wheel and gives an indication of the importance of the Abbey. The whole area of the Abbey has now been acquired by Manx National Heritage and is incorporated into the Story of Mann. Refer to Walk No.13.

Follow the boundary wall of the Abbey to the right and walk around the perimeter - you may be able to catch the odd glimpse of some of the remains through a gate on the way. Cross the road and almost opposite the waymarkers will direct you down a narrow lane and then left to the river again where you should turn right. The Way follows the river into Castletown on a pleasant walk through river meadows. Cross the river on a wooden bridge continuing on the other side of the river nearer to the steam railway. Look for the weir that took water from the river for the Golden Meadow Mill, which you will be able to see from the path as you pass Poulsom Park. The railway station is across the park and you can return to Douglas from there or continue into Castletown and finish your walk at the Castle.

WALK 23
RAAD NY FOILLAN

The coastal path was the ambition of Sir Ambrose Flux Dundas, who was a keen walker, and during his term of office as Governor of the Island attempts were made, at his instigation, to introduce legislation into the Island similar to the Parks and Countryside Act in the UK, but without success.

The first attempt at officially recording the Island's rights of way took place in the early 1950s based on research done during the period of the Second World War by R C W Brown, the then Surveyor General. A series of public meetings was held in the seventeen parishes of the Island, following which a report was submitted to Tynwald.

There the matter lay dormant until 1961 when the issue was tabled by John Quirk MHK member for Peel. The result was The Public Rights of Way Act 1961. The Definitive Maps were eventually deposited and gave legal authority to the network of rights of way enjoyed today.

It wasn't until the celebrations of the Millennium of Tynwald in 1979 that the opportunity to try and assemble a coastal path was considered. It wasn't complete then and isn't now, although little bits are still being added as the opportunity arises. For the present, sections of road have to be used between Glen Maye and Dalby and at Maughold.

The total length of the path is a little over 150km and for convenience it is divided into seven sections for a week's activity. Each section is a comfortable day walk with time to stop and admire the coastal scenery and bird-life of the Island. Public transport directions are given to and from Douglas as a starting point but the more adventurous can make arrangements for overnight accommodation at or near each of the section ends. It can be walked in five days by combining the first two sections and joining sections four and five.

SECTION 1: PEEL TO PORT ERIN

Take Bus No.5 or 6 to Peel to the stop by the House of Manannan from where the walk starts. It is a full day walk and you should allow 7 hours for the 24km.

Start by walking alongside the harbour to the bridge at the head of the harbour.

The coastal footpath was formally inaugurated in 1986 by the late Willie Quirk MHK, who was Chairman of the Highway Board which was the department of Government responsible for rights of way in the Island, and there is a small plaque to commemorate the event near the old water tank for the Railway that used to operate between Peel and Douglas (refer to The Heritage Trail). The site of the former railway station is now occupied by the House of Manannan which is operated by Manx National Heritage as part of The Story of Mann.

Cross the bridge at the head of the harbour and walk towards the Castle but after a short distance follow the broad track up the hill, being careful to take the grassy track sharp left at the corner as the Castle comes into view. You will soon see that there are two distinct parts to the hill that dominates Peel. The first is Peel Hill and the next part is Corrin's Hill surmounted by Corrin's Tower.

From the saddle between the two hills carry straight on to the summit of Corrin's Hill; or choose to take the path to the right that follows the old horse tramroad to the quarry on the back of Corrin's Hill. The latter is by far the more spectacular but the path is close to the cliff edge in places so care is needed, particularly with young children, and this is so for many places on the walk.

Whichever way you have chosen you will end up at the same spot overlooking the south west coast of the Island. Niarbyl *(literally meaning the tail - from the tail of rocks stretching out to sea)* is clearly seen. Cronk ny Arree Laa *(hill of the dawn)* dominates the skyline above with the hills stretching south to Fleshwick *(green creek)* and Bradda, with the Calf of Man just appearing in the far distance.

The path now becomes a real cliff path but it is easy to follow as it skirts the various bays and inlets. Look for Traie Cabbag *(cabbage shore - so named after the wild sea cabbage that grows there)* and the unusual rock known as the Bonnet Rock which is surrounded by water at most states of the tide. You will see why it has this local name when you find it.

Now as you approach Glen Maye *(yellow glen)* there is another choice. The path has to revert to the Coast road here as far as Dalby. You can follow the path down to the mouth of the glen as you round the headland and take the path up the opposite side of the glen to join the main road. Alternatively carry on down into the glen and follow the lower path, stopping to admire the waterfall before climbing the steps to the main road, and this is the preferred route. There is an opportunity here to break and use this section as a morning walk, taking the opportunity to lunch at Glen Maye before returning by public transport or walking back to Peel along the main road.

Turn right on reaching the coast road and follow it down the hill and up the other side of the glen to continue south parallel to and in sight of the coast all the way to Dalby *(glen farm)*. Deviate slightly from the official waymarked path because additional land has been acquired by Manx National Heritage and a section of coastal path hitherto not available for public use has also been dedicated.

Follow the signs down to the right to Niarbyl, where there is now a café and visitor centre and which is part of the Story of Mann. Continue towards the sea and here you will get your first view of Niarbyl point and the view south from here across what is known as the big bay towards Fleshwick and the Calf Island.

Walk up the track behind Florrie Forde's bungalow and follow the signs on this new section of the coastal path. After a short section following the edge of the cliff you will reach Traie Vane *(white beach)*. Here you can really see the dramatic way that Cronk ny Arrey Laa *(hill of the dawn)* sweeps down to the sea. Continue on the cliff path as far as the signpost directing you down the rough cut steps to the beach, making the last part of the descent over rough ground.

This is the beach which is referred to in the Bayr ny Skeddan Walk No.21, where the small fishing boats were hauled up on to the grass sward. Turn left and walk along the beach, looking for the signpost which will direct you up the track just after the waterfall and follow it up under the trees. Just above the beach house there is a commemorative seat bearing the inscription – 'sometimes I sits and thinks and sometimes I just sit' - why not pause and do just that, the view over Niarbyl Bay is worth it.

There is a fork in the path here. Be careful to go straight ahead and continue up the rough cut steps to the top and cross the hedge. Now anyone who hasn't a good head for heights should follow the green public right of way sign adjoining the field as far as the end stile which joins the 'slabs' and follow the track uphill. Continue straight ahead on Manx National Trust land and follow the broad track around the top of Gob ny Gameren *(probably from an obscure family name)* up to a stile which you should ignore and bear off to the right following a clear track.

The track skirts the top of Feustal *(precipice)* as far as the first zig-zag which we follow to the ladder stile over the wall. The Raad ny Foillan waymarker is reassuring. Carry straight on following the path on the edge of the cliff top. Extreme care is needed in places and the path has a severe cross fall which adds to the difficulty. Above Gob ny Ushtey *(headland of the waterfall - although the literal translation means beak of the water. The Manx often described headlands as looking like the bill or beak of a bird and so the description came into common use describing headlands)* the path swings inland to cross a stream and wall. Now start to head uphill in earnest, the path is distinct and there are signs at each of the crests. As the old farmhouse at Eary Cushlin *(Cosnahan's shieling)*, now a venture centre, comes into sight the going gets easier. Don't be deceived though, cross the track and continue uphill over the moorland, following the signs all the way to the top of Cronk ny Arrey Laa!

There are quite spectacular views all the way up the climb and at the summit you will be at the highest point on the coastal path. Take time out to admire the view back over Niarbyl towards Peel with Corrin's Tower visible in the far distance.

Now in the best tradition of what goes up must come down we make our way down towards the Sloc *(or Slough meaning pit or hollow)* over open moorland but following a clearly marked path. Flocks of choughs frequent this area and they are quite a distinctive bird with their bright red beaks and legs contrasting with their black plumage. They are now quite rare in the British Isles and the Island is one of its last refuges.

At the Sloc you leave the hill and join the road very briefly. Almost immediately you must enter back on to the moorland again by the picnic site on the other side of the boundary wall. Here, as so often with the coastal path, there are choices. The easy wide track to the left or the path to the right, which is for the more experienced walker and goes to the summit of Lhiattee ny Bienee *(literally meaning - summit on the side)* and over the Carnanes, commanding excellent views back towards Cronk ny Arrey Laa and the 'big bay' below.

Take the wide track and follow it to Surby *(a Norse word Saurbyr meaning moorland farm)*. Leaving the mountain it joins a surfaced road, which you should follow down to Surby. At Surby turn right and follow the road to Fleshwick *(green creek)* down the east side of the valley. As you approach the end of the valley look for the signs on the left of the road just after the farm which will take you over a stile to start a really steep climb that will take you to the top of Bradda.

Pause on the way up to admire the views behind you all the way up the coast to Niarbyl and across the valley at Fleshwick. Once over the top of this climb the view opens out in front of you down the coast to the Sound. This whole area was seriously affected by a deep-seated heath fire and it is taking time to recover.

The descent into Port Erin is easy and you will pass Milner's Tower on the way and here again you are faced with a number of alternative paths. Take the one following the coast through Bradda Glen and on to the upper Promenade at Port Erin. Walk into the village and follow the signs to the railway station and bus depot, from where there is a choice of transport back to Douglas.

If time is short, try this short walk based on Port Erin. Start from the railway station and cross the road into Bridson Street past the Cherry Orchard Hotel. Turn right into Bay View Road and left up Harrison Street and onto a Public Right of Way which will take you across the Rowany Golf Course. Be aware of golfers and keep an eye out for wayward golf balls! The path is clearly marked and the views are good. Keep heading for the valley ahead, avoiding the junctions with other paths and eventually emerge at Honna Hill crossing through an old stone-built stile in the boundary wall. Turn left and head up the hill to the top and look for the sign marking the Ernie Broadbent Walk off to the right. Follow this narrow road down the west side of the Fleshwick valley until joining the surfaced road to Fleshwick Beach just past the farm. Turn left and look for the signs showing where the Raad ny Foillan leaves the road a little distance further on and join the longer walk from Peel over Bradda and back to Port Erin.

SECTION 2: PORT ERIN TO PORT ST MARY

This is perhaps the most beautiful of all the Island walks, whatever the time of year and whatever the weather. It is approximately 18km in length. Allow about 4½ hours taking time to admire the views.

Take bus No.1 or No. 2 or the train to Port Erin where the walk for this section starts. Make your way from Station Road down to the lower Promenade and follow the sweep of the bay to the Albert Pier. At the start of the fishermen's stores on the left look for the flight of concrete steps up to the workshops at the higher level. These were the workshops used in connection with the ill-fated breakwater contract. The Port Erin breakwater contractors' tramway, described in the introduction, accessed the quarry area here and also the sheds. The arches over the present doors show where the rails entered the building.

Continue to the former Marine Biological Station opposite the root of the old breakwater. Look very carefully for the start of the next section of the coastal path as it has a very inauspicious start from behind an electrical sub-station!

Once on the path it is easy to follow, even if the stiff climb at the start is a little daunting. The path continues around the back of the old Marine Biological Station and up above Kione ny Garee *(literally meaning the end of the thicket)* where fulmars nest on the north-facing shaded cliffs throughout the year. The path levels out above Bay Fine and we have a good view back towards Port Erin and

Bradda Head. Care should be taken in windy conditions as the path is very exposed.

Around the next headland look out for an unusual finger of rock, known locally as Jacob's Rock, as you cross over the stile over a stone wall. The path passes close under the rock and you will cross a section of fissured rock as you skirt Aldrick *(old people's creek)* which you will see as you walk down towards the Sound. Ahead is the Calf of Man and the Sound with Kitterland and Thousla Rock. If you are at the right state of the tide you will see the tide race here and if it is at all stormy you will be treated to some spectacular sea views.

Cross the National Heritage car park, passing the Café and visitor centre (all described in Walk No.7).

The path skirts around Burroo Ned *(nest hill)* and you will see the back of Spanish Head above Baie ny Breechyn. Pass through a gate and cross a small stream to commence the very steep assault on the back of the Cronk Mooar *(big hill - although it has a local name of Cronk y Feeagh meaning hill of the raven, which is more appropriate as ravens do nest here).* This is the southernmost hill in the Island; not very high but you will know it is a hill after you have made the climb. Pause at the top and take in the views all round, over the Sound and the Calf of Man itself.

The path now starts to drop, still skirting the cliff edge, and then turns north to start its run up the east coast. The path is very close to the edge above Black Head and care should be taken, particularly with children. The path now starts to fall quickly towards Bay Stakka *(a corruption of Baie yn Stackey referring to the stack of Sugar Loaf Rock)* which it skirts and then climbs to the Chasms, which are on the right. Again the path is exposed at this point and care should be taken before crossing the wall on a substantial stile heading towards the derelict building that was formerly a cafe.

Go through the wooden gate and follow the waymarked route alongside the wall on your left. This should avoid having to cross any of the Chasms, which are deep clefts in the rock and quite an unusual phenomenon. Be careful to descend the path, keeping close to the wall on the left all the way to a metal kissing-gate above Cashtal Kione ny Goagyn *(meaning the castle of chasms head)* or Sugar Loaf Rock as it is more popularly known because of its unusual shape. It is inhabited by colonies of guillemots, kittiwakes and fulmars with the occasional razorbill and sometimes puffins and this is perhaps the most spectacular view of the rock, providing you have a good head for heights.

The path crosses the next field diagonally, heading for a gap in the stone wall opposite. Before leaving the cliff edge you can just catch a glimpse of 'the anvil' or as it is sometimes called 'the pulpit rock' which is a rock standing clear of the cliff in the small bay behind the Sugar Loaf Rock. From the sea it looks like an anvil but from above it looks like a pulpit with an open bible on it.

Follow the well-defined track between walls eventually leading onto a surfaced road to Glenchass *(an English corruption of Glion Shast meaning sedge glen)* and Port St Mary. Take the right fork at Glenchass and follow the road downhill for a short distance, looking for a sign on the right. Follow the path down to the shoreline at Perwick *(harbour creek).* The route follows the beach at Perwick and Traie Coon *(narrow beach)* before swinging up a zig-zag path from the stony shoreline to join the path beside the Golf Course and on to Port St Mary Promenade.

Walk along the sea wall, passing a disused limekiln and the breakwater into Lime Street and the inner harbour. Port St. Mary remains largely unspoilt but is now occupied by pleasure-craft rather than commercial fishing boats.

Turn left at the end of Lime Street and then right to follow the lower promenade and join the Cain Karran elevated walkway which gives an impressive entrance into Chapel Bay, without doubt one of the Island's prettiest and most sheltered bays. Walk up into the village where there is a choice of places to eat and from where it is possible to catch a bus or train back to Douglas.

SECTION 3: PORT ST MARY TO DOUGLAS

This walk is a full day walk of 30km for which you should allow 8 hours. Take public transport to Port St Mary: if by bus (No.1, No. 11 or No. 12) get off at the harbour, or if by train there is a short walk from the station to the village.

The path continues around the Lower Promenade and Gansey Point to Bay ny Carrickey *(bay of the rock)* following the coast road to Fishers Hill for approximately 2km. Pass the gatehouses and boundary wall to Kentraugh House and you may just catch a glimpse of this fine mansion where there is a break in the windswept trees that form the boundary.

Continue along the sea wall and take the right fork at the bottom of the Fishers Hill to follow the single track surfaced road almost on the shore line to Poolyvaaish *(poyll vaaish literally meaning the pool of death. The origin of the name is obscure but one likely explanation is that a slaughter house associated with the farm may have drained into one of the many sea pools).* The whole area teems with birdlife and you should particularly look for herons who patiently fish in the rock pools and on the edge of the water competing with the curlew and the oyster-catchers. The path continues through the farm buildings at Pooylvaaish and round the low headland beside the quarry from which the black limestone for the steps of St. Pauls Cathedral in London was obtained. Cross the stone stile over the wall to open onto the grassy headland at Scarlett *(cormorant's cleft).*

The path follows the edge of the fields skirting the rocks which change dramatically, showing their volcanic origin and culminating in the stack known as Scarlett, which is a volcanic plug to a vent long-since extinct. The broken jagged rocks are the remains of an ancient volcanic lava flow. The rock changes from basalt to limestone as you approach Castletown, the ancient capital of the Island dominated by its magnificent castle.

Enter the town square and turn right to skirt the Castle, passing the police station and immediately turning right again, then left over the footbridge to cross the harbour. Turn right into Douglas Street and past the Nautical Museum, which together with the Castle is also part of the Story of Mann, both having interesting presentations.

Continue along Douglas Street and right into College Green, then follow the promenade towards King William's College and the airport. Carry on as far as Derbyhaven, turning left along the road to the end. At the entrance to the flying club look for the waymarkers which will take you around the edge of the airport boundary and under the approach lights gantry. A proposal to lengthen the main runway will almost certainly affect the route of the path here so there will no doubt be a diversion on completion.

Climb onto an ancient raised beach which you should follow to Cass ny Hawin *(the foot of the river)* where the Santon river joins the sea through a dramatic gorge. The gorge was cut by the melt water from the retreating ice sheet during the Ice Age. There is a commanding view of the gorge from the site of an ancient Bronze Age fort. The route of the glacial retreat can be traced all the way to Granite Mountain near Foxdale.

The path now follows the gorge inland until you come to a bridge crossing the river and then returns to the coast down the other side of the gorge. Although signposted it is often wet and difficult underfoot despite the provision of raised footboards. Once back on the coast again the path is easy to follow along the top of the cliffs. You will be rewarded with good views all the way north towards Douglas. The next bay you will come to is Port Soldrick *(sunny creek).*

Just where the path turns inland to drop

Santon Gorge

down to the shoreline look across the bay at the large caves in the opposite headland and the view of the coast north towards the flat top of Santon Head. The coastal path descends to the beach for a short distance before climbing back up the opposite side of the bay to continue along the cliff top.

The next inlet is Port Grenaugh and the path again descends onto the shore. Continue across the front of the sea wall and follow the signpost leading up to a stile across a wall and climb up the other side of the bay. Look for the promontory fort and Viking settlement at Cronk ny Merrui *(literally the hill of the dead people)* on the right as you climb. Continuing along the coast pass Purt Veg *(little port)* where you will walk on the top of the old field boundary hedge around the rim of the bay.

Continue on, ignoring the junction of another path to Meary Vooar and cross the small stream on the footbridge. A short climb brings you back on to the cliff edge which you should follow to the next inlet and as you turn inland look across at the opposite head with the cave running through it. This is the Baltic Rock and there are three caves intersecting it. You have to climb down one side and scramble up the other to regain the path on towards Santon Head. Can you see the rock that portrays the head of Queen Victoria looking out to sea?

Now you are passing close to the Island's central sewage disposal works but they are well screened by the bank of the nearby new firing range on land at Meary Veg. Cross a muddy section before commencing the climb up to the headland at Ballnahowe *(an obscure meaning but roughly translated means farm of the headland)*. Care needs to be taken here as the path follows the top of an old hedge which has been broken down by cattle and it can be a hazard in summer when the overgrowth of gorse obscures the path.

At the top you will see Pistol Castle below and the cliffs at Ballacregga with the Marine Drive beyond. Unfortunately you have to turn inland here as this short section of the coast to Port Soderick does not have a coastal path and there is no alternative other than to follow the signpost and head inland. Cross the field and enter a farm occupation road as far as the surfaced road to Ballnahowe Farm where you should turn left and follow the road to the Old Castletown Road. The single track road crosses the steam railway before joining the Old Castletown Road and on the left there was a wayside halt for many years which was used by those accessing the old firing range at Ballnahowe.

At the main road turn right and follow the road for a little over 2km - take care as there is no footway. Descending Crogga Hill *(from the Norse Krok-a meaning winding river)* you pass Crogga House and its decorative lake before seeing a waymarker which will direct you down towards Port Soderick *(has the same meaning as Soldrick – sunny or south facing creek)* passing under the steam railway.

Keep to the road and take the left fork along the Marine Drive that you will now follow along the coast, passing the inlet at Keristal *(rock farm)*. The coastal path now follows the route of the former Marine Drive tramway all the way to Douglas (refer to Walk No.8 and the introduction for the full description). Note the change again in the rock formations with the contorted strata now in fragmented slate clearly visible in the cliffs all around you. Problems with the cliff faces have meant that the road is closed to through traffic but cars are able to use most of it, so be aware. Approaching the old toll gate house means that you are almost at Douglas and rounding the corner there is the whole of the bay spread out before you.

The coastal path now descends the steps between the lighthouse and the now-restored Camera Obscura down to the breakwater where you should follow the harbour past the Lifeboat House. The Douglas Lifeboat is appropriately named Sir William Hillary after the founder of the Royal National Lifeboat Institution who lived in Douglas in the early part of the nineteenth century. Cross the lift bridge and finish the walk at the Sea Terminal.

SECTION 4: DOUGLAS TO LAXEY

This is a good half-day walk with Laxey as its destination where there is a good choice of places to have lunch and spend the afternoon in the Laxey Wheel area enjoying a look at the Island's rich industrial past. Allow 4 hours for the 15km walk.

Starting at the Sea Terminal on the Loch Promenade, walk along the Loch Promenade walkway which was built in the 1870s to enclose part of the foreshore and extend the lower part of Douglas. Some of the original Victorian façade is now giving way to modern development and illustrates dramatically the changing face of Douglas. It is still possible to get a flavour of the grand Victorian façade of the promenade as you make your way north.

Stop opposite the Sefton Hotel to admire its elevation and that of the Gaiety Theatre. The church to the left and set back off the promenade was completed in 1849 and dedicated to St Thomas, the patron Saint of Architecture. It was designed by Ewan Christian RIBA an architect of Manx descent who was Architect to the Church Commissioners (1814 - 1895) and noted particularly for his work at Carlisle Cathedral. The building work was undertaken by local contractor Richard Cowle. It was built to serve the needs of an expanding town and the arrival of the tourist development along Loch Promenade led to it being referred to as 'the visitor's church'.

A fire in the tower in 1912 destroyed the bells and the organ that had been built and installed in 1886 by William Hill of London. The fire damage was repaired and a new peal of bells was installed five months later. At the same time the organ was repaired and enlarged, providing the Island with what is considered to be the finest instrument in the Island.

Continuing to the end of the promenade modern redevelopment is more apparent as old boarding houses are being replaced with modern apartments, reflecting a changing way of life in the island. At the bottom of Summerhill, pass the stables for the unique Douglas Bay Horse Tramway which dates from 1876. The depot where the horsecars are kept is at the end of Strathallan Crescent and also adjoins the terminus of the Electric Tramway which runs between Douglas and Ramsey and which commenced operation in 1895. Both tramways still operate and utilise original equipment, making them a mecca for transport enthusiasts the world over.

Continue past Port Jack and around the loop of Seaview Road, admiring the coastal views which now appear with the houses overlooking Douglas Bay. Joining the Coast Road again look for the waymarker that will direct you along the cliff top, past new apartments built on the site of the former Majestic Hotel and almost through the front gardens of houses on King Edward Road before joining the road again at Lag Birragh *(literally the sharp pointed hollow - referring to the rocks below)*. The path continues along King Edward Road to Groudle *(narrow glen)* where you should follow the waymarkers directing you down to the shore by the holiday homes. Cross the river by the footbridge and climb up the path opposite to cross the Groudle Glen Railway, which was a Victorian novelty now restored and operated by enthusiasts throughout the summer months.

Follow the path upwards and on to a narrow surfaced single track road, looking for a waymarker to direct you across the fields to Garwick. On the way look for the signpost to Lonan Old Church and take time to make a detour to see it and the standing Celtic Wheel Cross in the grounds.

Walk through the fields until the path joins Clay Head Road, which you should follow towards Baldrine. Keep a look out for the waymarker directing you off to the right to Garwick beach and follow the fisherman's path to the shore and then immediately go all the way back up the other side of the glen, following the signs to join the main road again.

Turn right at the top and continue towards Laxey, no pavement again so be careful, following the tramway. At Fairy Cottage there is an option if the tide is out! At low water you can take another fisherman's path down onto the beach and walk to Laxey harbour, which gives a lovely entry into Laxey. Otherwise you must continue down Old Laxey Hill into Old Laxey and the harbour.

Follow Glen Road to Laxey Village and up the hill under the church to the centre of the village. Christ Church, Laxey is situated in what must be a unique setting for any church and its history is entwined with the mining history of Laxey (see Walk No.4). It is not surprising that we find that the Laxey Mining Company and one of its principal shareholders G W Dumbell was instrumental in promoting a church for the village. Part of the garden of the Mines Captains House was made available for the church to be built right

Laxey harbour

in the middle of the village.

There is plenty to see in Laxey before returning to Douglas by public transport.

SECTION 5: LAXEY TO RAMSEY

Allow 6 hours for this 20km walk which starts from Laxey tram station in the heart of Laxey Village, convenient to either bus or tram from Douglas.

Leave the station by the path alongside the station building and walk down to Captains Hill, turning right to join Glen Road opposite St. George's Woollen Mills and make your way to the harbour. Look for the large factory-type building on the opposite side of the river. This was built as the power generating station for the Laxey section of the Manx Electric Railway.

At the junction by the harbour bridge look to the opposite side of the road for the waymarker for the coastal path which you should follow up an old packhorse road to Ballaragh *(of doubtful origin best seen as derived from Balley arraght meaning farm of the spectre or apparition)* being careful crossing the main coast road. Continue up to join the Ballaragh Road which we follow through Ballaragh to the top of the hill, where views open towards Maughold Head and across the Irish Sea to Cumbria and the Lake District.

The road curves away from the coast and starts to drop downhill. Look for the waymarker on the corner that you should follow over the fence and diagonally down through the fields. Cross the main road again and the tram track with care and continue on the public right of way until it joins the Dhoon Glen Loop Road. Cross one stile on to the road and then immediately back over the adjacent stile to follow the track down to sea level again. It is worth the effort, even though this is another of those down and back up again detours.

The path skirts the Dhoon Glen and you will catch a glimpse of the wheel case of the Dhoon Rhennie Mine *(Dhoon is derived probably from an Irish word meaning fort and rhenny is a ferny place)* which operated to extract lead and zinc but was not productive and eventually abandoned. Then the mouth of the glen opens up and you will have a view of the headland of Kion e Hennin *(Kione ny eaynin headland of the cliff. Kione literally means beak or bill of a bird as mentioned before but by common usage has come to mean headland)* with its inclined grey slate which is the native rock of the area. Immediately behind this headland there was a granite boss which for years was quarried for its pink Granite.

The path drops to the shore and then returns behind the picnic table. Follow the path within the glen, climbing past the Island's most spectacular waterfall which is made up of three falls which empty into a pool beside the path. A further steep climb will take you back to the point where you began this detour.

Turn right on to the Dhoon Loop Road and follow it over the tramway back to the main road and turn right. Almost immediately turn right again and at the bottom of the hill turn right yet again to Cornaa, making sure to take the right fork by the ford, following the single track road down to Cornaa *(an ancient treen - land division- name)*.

You are now back at sea level again, but this time with a difference. Behind the shingle bank is a saltmarsh with an attendant variety of birdlife. The path crosses the river and follows an unsurfaced road, known as Benussi's lane, all the way up the right-hand side of the valley heading inland. Cross the tramway again and the main road to continue up the Raad ny Quakerin *(the Quaker's road)* pausing to look at the Quakers burial ground at the summit.

Descending through Ballajora *(farm of the strangers)* there is a view of Maughold Head and the lighthouse. At the bottom of the hill look for the signs directing you to the right to Port Mooar *(the great harbour)*. Follow the path round the coast, through the tall grass to Gob ny Rona *(headland of the seals)* where you may very well see some seals. At Dhyrnane you will pass some derelict workings from an iron ore mine before climbing away from the shore. Cross some fields past a lime kiln to join the road to the lighthouse, turning right for a short distance before turning left onto Maughold Brooghs. Follow the path over the headland, past more old mine workings at Gob Ago *(literally edge headland)* before joining the road again and turning right towards Ramsey.

As before, you will have more choices; you can carry on into Ramsey along the main road but again if the tide is out you can go down the slip at Port e Vullen *(harbour of the mill)* onto the shore and follow the cliff path around the headland at Tableland to rejoin the road again a little further on.

Either way it is back up to the main road, passing Belle Vue tram stop to follow the main road again all the way down to Ramsey. At Ballure *(Balley euar meaning yew tree estate or farm)* it is possible to make a detour into Ballure Glen and to Ramsey along the beach, but this latter option is only available at low water. Make your way into Ramsey along the promenade as far as the church of St. Maughold and Our Lady Star of the Sea at the end of the promenade which was built in 1900 and designed by Giles Gilbert Scott. Turn left into St Paul's Square to finish this section of the walk.

Return to Douglas either by tram or bus from the tram station in Waterloo Road.

SECTION 6: RAMSEY TO BALLAUGH

This walk is also part of the Coastal Footpath and is by way of a complete contrast, embracing the northern alluvial plain. It is also the longest section, being almost 30km long and is definitely a full day walk.

The walk is very dependent on tidal conditions and should not be undertaken when the tide is rising. The ideal start is shortly after high water, although there are alternatives which avoid the risk areas.

Starting from the tram station, which is also close to the bus station, make your way to St Paul's Square and follow the quayside to the swing bridge and cross to the Mooragh Promenade *(Mooragh meaning waste land by the sea)* and then follow the promenade as far as the Vollan. Here is where the first choice has to be made, which is entirely dependent on the tide. If the tide is out, then it is possible to walk all the way to the Point of Ayre on the shingle beach. If not, then I'm afraid that there is no alternative other than to walk up the hill, turn right and follow the road to Bride Village and onward to the Point of Ayre.

Now the geology of the cliffs has changed once more and they are all sand. The high cliffs at Shelag *(here the original Norse name means seal creek or bay)* are quite dramatic but because of erosion the bay no longer exists. The whole area continues to be subject to storm erosion as you will clearly see as you continue along the shore as far as the Phurt *(port)*. From the Phurt follow the raised beach which clearly illustrates the glacial formation of the northern plain. The whole of the Ayres was formed by alluvial deposit and here the terrain changes yet again with shingle underfoot all the way around the northernmost tip of the Island.

The lighthouse which marks the northernmost tip of the island was designed by Robert Stevenson and built by the Commissioners of Northern Lights in 1818. The shingle is constantly on the move, as can be seen by the smaller additional lighthouse that was added seventy-two years after the original. Like almost all the lighthouses around the coast of the British Isles, it is no longer manned but is controlled from a remote central station in Scotland.

Continue round the coast on the shoreline, which is heavy going underfoot but worth it for the wild natural beauty to seaward with birdlife in abundance. Look for gannets with their spectacular diving and their vivid white that sets them apart from all the other birds. Curious seals will often follow you as you make your way along the beach. You will also be accompanied by the vivid black and white oyster-catchers with their red beaks and shrill calls, but you will never get near to them as they will constantly leapfrog you.

Passing Rue Point and Blue Point where the rifle range and the old Coastguard lookout are located, you will be back into sand. The whole of the northern plain has been drained by successive generations to bring back into use many acres of fertile agricultural land. The last major undertaking was the formation of a lengthy drainage channel which discharges at the Lhen *(Lhen Mooar - meaning great ditch)*. When you reach there the Lhen Trench discharges across the shore and wading is the only way to get across, so its boots off and round the neck.

Approaching Jurby Head, the sand cliffs are back with a vengeance and continue almost to Peel. At Jurby Head, if the tide is well out, look for the remains of the trawler Passages which was driven ashore in 1929 in a north-west gale, becoming a total loss, the crew being successfully rescued by the rocket brigade of the day.

You will have walked far enough by now on sand and shingle, which is not the easiest of going, and the locals have a saying 'two steps forward one step back' which sums up beach walking admirably. After passing Jurby Head, approach the Killane *(from the Scandinavian Kjarrland meaning Brushwood land)* where another drainage ditch discharges to the sea. Look for the signs shortly after here where the Ballaugh shore road joins the shoreline at the Cronk.

Leave the shore and walk to Ballaugh Village, passing the old parish Church of St Mary de Ballaugh dating from the middle of the eighteenth century. It is noted for its leaning gate pillars, which by reference to photographs and old guides must have been like that for a hundred years at least.

Walking towards Ballaugh, admire the backdrop of the western hills and see the tower of the new Parish Church which you pass as you enter the village. Work on building the church commenced in May 1830. Many of the older parish churches were all located more or less centrally in the various parishes. As communities developed in the villages these churches were often too far from the people they were supposed to serve. Ballaugh was no exception although the old church was also considered too small as well too far from the centre of population; even though it was no more than a mile away near the coast.

The Church, designed by Hanson and Welch, is built in local stone in a style unique amongst Island churches. The tall lancet-type windows and intervening buttresses to the nave and the ornate pinnacles make it quite distinctive.

You will arrive in the centre of the village opposite the public house and beside the world famous Ballaugh Bridge, very much part of the TT course. Return to Douglas or Ramsey by public transport.

SECTION 7: BALLAUGH TO PEEL

Allow 5 hours for this walk of almost 22km, which is all easy going. Take public transport to Ballaugh (Buses: No. 5, No. 5c, No. 6 or No. 6a) and start the walk from the centre of the village.

Leave the village by Station Road and walk to the Cronk, passing the two churches described in the previous section. On the way pass the Dollagh and again as in all Manx place names there is more to the name than meets the eye. Much of the northern plain in early times was flooded and the land was covered with several large lakes. There are no visible signs of these lakes left now except in times of heavy rainfall when remnants appear here and there. Dollagh is a corruption of Doufloch *(black lake)* other places like Ellan Rhenny *(ferny island)* and Ellan Bane *(white island)* and even the parish name of Ballaugh *(a corruption of Balley ny Loughey - lake farm)* gives a clue to what this area was like in early times.

At the Cronk turn left and follow the Bollyn *(Boayl ein - spot of the birds)* Road as far as the Orrisdale Road. There are good views of the western hills which form the backdrop to Bishopscourt, the ancient seat of the Bishop of Sodor and Mann but now a private residence. Turn right at the junction with the Orrisdale Road and follow the road through Orrisdale *(from the Scandinavian Orrastaor meaning estate of the moorfowl)* Look for the signpost at the corner after the farm which leads to the shore at Glen Trunk. Go through the gate and follow the wide grassy track to the shore, passing one of the best preserved lime kilns on the Island.

Once at the shore you can see Peel in the distance so turn left and walk along the shore flanked by steep sand cliffs and you will see that these are also subject to erosion and for that reason it is not advisable to walk close underneath them. You will notice here that in addition to the oyster-catchers, herring gulls and black-backed gulls you will be accompanied by flocks of curlew which graze the foreshore and live on the hill slopes of the western hills. Ringed plover are often seen in this area and the occasional chough.

As you approach Glen Wyllin *(glen of the mill)* there are some sea defence works on the foreshore, which is a recent attempt to slow down the rate of erosion. Walk past these and a short distance further along the shoreline look for the signpost directing you off the shore at Glen Mooar *(the great glen)*.

Leave the shore here and make your way up the narrow surfaced road to the main coast road. Look across the road and you will see a waymarker directing you into the glen. Follow the path as far as the stone pier, which is one of two piers that carried the railway across the glen on lattice steel girders. Climb (see Walk No.20) the roughly-cut steps up the side of the embankment to join the disused railway track that now forms part of the coastal path for the next three miles as far as the old station at St. German's Halt.

If you look back from the elevated position once on the track you will immediately get an impression of just how severe the erosion of the sand cliffs is at this point. In places it will not be long before the coast road will be threatened and this is the point where the natural gas supply pipe enters the island! There are a couple of farm crossings before you approach a rock cutting at Skerisdale *(or more correctly Skeresstaor from the Norse meaning rocky farm)*. This was another place which was bad to trap snow whenever the winter was really bad. The railway now runs closer to the sea than the road; imagine just how dramatic the journey by train was as it clung to the cliffs and spanned the glens on viaducts and embankments.

Leaving the cutting the track-bed emerges onto one of those embankments as it spans Glion Cam *(the winding glen)* and opens up views of Peel and the Castle on St. Patrick's Isle in the distance. The coast road can be seen to the left and above as it winds its way around the head of the glen, giving it the local name of the Devil's Elbow.

After a further half mile in a shallow cutting, which is sometimes quite wet and muddy, the path emerges into the open and now really does cling to the cliff. When the railway was still operating, this section, known as the 'donkey bank', gave continuous problems with settlement, immediately apparent as you walk across it. Looking below, the rocks are back on the shore line at Gob y Deigan as you cross the second of the embankments. From here the physical features of the coast change yet again from the sand cliffs to slate and then to red sandstone as you get nearer to Peel.

The path continues on the track-bed for a further mile, crossing yet another glen on an embankment at Glion Booigh *(the dirty glen)*. It is worth stopping on the embankment to look down at the trees growing in this glen. There is a great variety with some surprises and in many ways it is one of the unspoilt corners of the Island and only really appreciated from this location. The path now curves left to join the coast road at the site of the former St. German's Halt with the old station building and gatehouse still just recognisable for what they were.

Leave the track here and follow the road for a short distance downhill and round the corner at the bottom. Look for the signpost on the right after the corner and go through the kissing-gate to join the headland path. The path climbs some rough cut steps and reaches a promontory above Cass Struan *(stream end)*. Stop and look north back along the route that you have just walked and observe the sand cliffs stretching all the way north to the prominent white outline of Jurby Church and Jurby Head in the distance. Now look below and there is the sandstone to which I referred which outcrops here in a glorious burst of russet red.

The path now continues to Peel along the headland path above Traie Fogog *(or more correctly Traie Feoghaig - meaning periwinkle shore)* commanding the best views over Peel and the Castle. Continue along the defined path above the old swimming pool and descend down into the town and the Promenade. There are several places to take refreshment and any of the roads off the promenade lead to the town centre and the town hall for return to Douglas.

Looking over the north of Island from North Burrule

USEFUL INFORMATION

The information given in this alphabetical listing, relevant to many of the articles in the guide, is useful for checking out opening times, admission prices, what's on and other details which can help you to plan and make the most of your visit to the Isle of Man.

ARTS & ENTERTAINMENT

■ Villa Marina & Gaiety Theatre Complex. Enquiries 01624 694566. Box office 01624 694555. ***www.villamarina.com***

■ Arts Council (for details of what's on and to obtain a copy of the Ten-Year Strategy). 10 Villa Marina Arcade, Douglas. 01624 611316. ***www.gov.im/artscouncil***

BUS AND TRAIN SERVICES

■ For up-to-date timetable and fare information, contact Isle of Man Transport on 01624 662525 or the Tourist Information Centre on 01624 686766.

FERRY SERVICES

For details of routes, services, fares and special offers contact the Steam Packet on 01624 661661 or visit ***www.steam-packet.com***

FURTHER READING

■ Other books published by Lily Publications:

Visions of Mann
Train & Trams of the Isle of Man
Trains of the Isle of Man
Wildlife of the Isle of Man
Wild Flowers of Mann
Steam Packet in Camera
Ferries of the Isle of Man

Laxey harbour

Steam Packet 175
King Orry III

These titles are all available direct from Lily Publications at PO Box 33, Ramsey, Isle of Man IM99 4LP. Tel: 01624 898446. Fax: 01624 898449. Email: ***sales@lilypublications.co.uk***

Website: ***www.lilypublications.co.uk***

HARBOURS

■ ***Douglas***. Good shelter except in NE winds, very heavy seas in NE gales. Harbour Master 01624 686627.

■ ***Laxey***. Sheltered except in strong NE/SE winds. Harbour dries out. Port Manager 01624 861663.

■ ***Peel***. Good shelter except in strong NW to NE winds, when entry should not be attempted. Harbour Office 01624 842338.

■ ***Port St Mary***. Very good shelter except in E or SE winds. Inner harbour dries out. Port Manager (also for Port Erin and Castletown) 01624 833206.

■ ***Ramsey***. Very good shelter except in strong NE/SE winds. Harbour dries out. Port Manager 01624 812245.

ISLE OF MAN LAW

The Isle of Man has a strong anti-drugs policy and illegal possession of banned substances can lead to imprisonment.

ISLE OF MAN WEBSITES

The main visitor website gives details of accommodation, events, attractions, activities, TT and motorsport, travel information, special offers and more. Visit ***www.visitisleofman.com***

The Isle of Man Government website at ***www.gov.im*** has a comprehensive index and is also a mine of information.

LICENSING LAWS

Liberal new Isle of Man legislation has introduced 24-hour opening for pubs, bars and off-licences. This means that all licensed premises, including nightclubs, restaurants and the Douglas casino, now have the option to serve alcohol 24 hours a day but only within their stated pre-arranged opening times.

MANX NATIONAL HERITAGE

■ For opening times, admission prices (where applicable) and other information about Manx National Heritage sites call 01624 648000. Or visit ***www.gov.im/mnh*** or either of the Isle of Man websites.

MANX WILDLIFE TRUST

Manx Wildlife Trust is based at the Tynwald Mills Centre in St John's. The shop here has a wealth of leaflets, books, maps and other information about Isle of Man wildlife and habitats. Call 01624 801985 or visit ***www.wildlifetrust.org.uk/manxwt***

MOTORING LAWS AND INFORMATION

■ ***Careful drivers***. Isle of Man roads and lanes are narrow and should be negotiated with care.

■ ***Mobile phones***. It is an offence to use a hand-held mobile phone while driving.

■ ***Parking discs***. These are required in some of the larger towns and villages and are available **free** from Isle of Man Steam Packet vessels, the Sea Terminal, airport, car hire companies and local Commissioners Offices.

■ ***Seatbelts***. Similar seatbelt laws to those in the UK and elsewhere apply.

■ ***Trailer caravans*** are not permitted on the Isle of Man without a permit, but tenting campers and self-propelled motor caravans are welcome.

TOURIST WELCOME CENTRE

■ Address: Sea Terminal, Douglas, Isle of Man IM1 2RG.

■ Telephone: 01624 686766.

■ Open throughout the year: April-September 7 days a week, October-March Monday to Friday.

TOURIST INFORMATION POINTS

Open all year:

■ Airport 01624 821600
■ Castletown 01624 825005
■ Onchan 01624 621228
■ Peel 01624 842341
■ Port Erin 01624 832298 & 835858
■ Port St Mary 01624 832101
■ Ramsey 01624 817025

Summer only:

■ Ballasalla 01624 822531
■ Laxey Heritage Trust 01624 862007